Speaking and Listening

Andrew Hammond

CONTENTS

HOW TO USE MIND'S EYE SPEAKING and LISTENING

'Communication is crucial.'

'The ability to communicate is an essential life skill for all children and young people in the twenty-first century. It is at the core of all social interaction. With effective communication skills, children can engage and thrive. Without them, children will struggle to learn, achieve, make friends and interact with the world around them.'

These words are taken from the latest report on the Speech, Language and Communication needs of children and young people from 0-19 years. (The Bercow Report DCSF-00632-2008).

The Mind's Eye speaking and listening packs offer teachers exciting and engaging ways to develop the speaking and listening skills necessary for life and learning. As a parent of a five year old child said in the report: *"Speech, language and communication is the most important thing in all our children ... It's their key to life"*

Prepare

- Photocopy the student activity sheet (photocopymaster).
- Bring up the image and 'hide' using the hide and reveal tool on your interactive whiteboard.
- Read the teacher's notes.

Introduce the lesson

- Follow the step-by-step instructions at the top of the Teacher's Notes page. This will help to orientate the children to the image and support the later work.

Choose and deliver an activity/series of activities

- Choose either **Speaking**, **Listening**, **Group Discussion** or **Drama**.
- Follow the instructions for each activity or use them as a jumping off point for your own ideas for group work.
- Extend the students by using the Extension section at the bottom of the page.

Set a practice, assessment or homework piece of work

- Use the photocopymaster to lead this activity to elicit specific responses or to support planning and development of written and spoken English ideas.

PRIMARY NATIONAL STRATEGY FRAMEWORK FOR LITERACY
www.standards.dcsf.gov.uk/primaryframework/literacy

TEACHING OBJECTIVES COVERED IN MIND'S EYE YEAR 4

SPEAKING	• Offer reasons and evidence for their views, considering alternative opinions • Respond appropriately to the contributions of others in the light of differing viewpoints • Tell stories effectively and convey detailed information coherently for listeners • Use and reflect on some ground rules for sustaining talk and interactions
LISTENING	• Listen to a speaker, make notes on the talk and use notes to develop a role-play • Compare the different contributions of music, words and images in short extracts from TV programmes • Identify how talk varies with age, familiarity, gender and purpose
GROUP DISCUSSION	• Take different roles in groups and use the language appropriate to them, including the roles of leader, reporter, scribe and mentor • Use time, resources and group members efficiently by distributing tasks, checking progress and making back-up plans • Identify the main points of each speaker, compare their arguments and how they are presented
DRAMA	• Create roles showing how behaviour can be interpreted from different viewpoints • Develop scripts based on improvisation • Comment constructively on plays and performances, discussing effects and how they are achieved

PLANNING FOR SPEAKING & LISTENING (YEAR 4)

In a useful handbook entitled *Speaking, Listening, Learning: working with children in Key Stages 1 and 2*, the DfES (2003) define the contexts, purposes and experiences needed for children to develop as effective speakers and learners in the following way:

Speaking: being able to speak clearly and to develop and sustain ideas in talk;

Listening: developing active listening strategies and critical skills of analysis;

Group discussion: taking different roles in groups, making a range of contributions and working collaboratively;

Drama: improvisation and working in role, scripting and performing, and responding to performances.

MAKING PROGRESS

Speaking

Can the pupils:

- take a long turn spontaneously?
- give a clear account/explanation which is sustained and complete?
- use presentational techniques such as gestures and visual aids?
- use formal language appropriately?

Listening

Can the pupils:

- listen attentively in discussion by following up points, agreeing or disagreeing with other speakers?
- use background knowledge about speakers to focus their listening purposefully?
- identify in broadcasts some of the presentational features used in shaping and organising meanings?

Group discussion

Can the pupils:

- use talk to plan and organise work in a group?
- participate in group work where the tasks are both speculative and practical?
- work in groups of different sizes, taking different roles?
- sustain group work over time, organising group members and resources?

Drama

Can the children:

- improvise dialogue and events to interpret key ideas and issues?
- perform plays to engage the interests of an audience in school?
- compare and comment constructively on the success of different performances?

ASSESSING AND RECORDING

To be able to trace pupils' progress effectively, follow these guidelines:

Make notes: much of the pupils' learning in speaking and listening takes place spontaneously, as comments are exchanged and ideas shared within paired and group discussions. Keep a 'talk diary' in which you can record notable comments made by pupils in the course of a Mind's Eye activity

Take digital photograph: whenever possible, take digital photos of specific children involved in Mind's Eye activities. These could form a useful display to raise the status of speaking and listening activities in class.

Set goals: prior to a Mind's Eye activity, select specific targets drawn from the 'Making Progress' sections above and express them to the children, e.g. 'This time, let's focus on using gestures when we talk.'

Encourage self-evaluation: encourage the children to keep a record of their own progress in speaking and listening by

evaluating their own performance in Mind's Eye activities, using a record sheet or 'talk diary' of their own.

Share successes: at the end of a particularly effective session, share ideas and elicit the children's own views about how they contributed and why the session was successful.

Record performances: using video cameras and/or audio equipment, record discussions and oral presentations. Play back and evaluate together.

Arrange 'assessed' activities: choose a specific Mind's Eye activity and explain to the class that it will be used as an assessment so they understand that for in this particular activity you will be scoring the contributions made by each pupil. Plan to cover one activity from Speaking, Listening, Group Discussion and Drama over the course of the book (taken from a variety of different units).

TEACHER'S NOTES

Introduction

- Load up the Mind's Eye CD-ROM. You may like to tell the children what the title of the session is before you reveal the image, or just open up the picture and watch their initial reactions to it.

- With the whole image in view, elicit the children's first impressions, recording their words on a mind-map on the board. These initial words and phrases will help to establish what is happening and describe the drama, i.e. *rescue, airlift, SOS, army helicopter, casualty.*

Familiarisation

- Elicit the children's prior knowledge of such air rescues: where do they normally take place? Good answers are *off the coast, on mountains, traffic laden areas in cities.*

- Look together at the image and try to establish more about the scene from clues: e.g. *camouflaged paint on helicopter suggests military aircraft, white chalk cliffs suggest coastal rescue, stretcher suggests severely injured person.*

Exploration

- Explore key words and phrases to describe the emotions felt by both the injured person and the aircrew. Brainstorm these on the board, as the children explore the scene in their mind's eye (e.g. *concerned, worried, relieved, vulnerable, serious condition, courageous*).

- Invite the children to suggest proper scenarios for this image, such as how, why, where and when this incident takes place.

UH 1H Iroquois helicopter airlifts injured patient.
© Brand X Pictures/Alamy

ACTIVITIES

Speaking

- **Telephone conversations:** Ask the children to work in pairs. The children perform an improvised telephone conversation, sitting back to back, in which one person recalls the air rescue from the viewpoint of an eyewitness walking along the cliff top. The other person must react to their comments and ask appropriate questions.

- **Talking pairs:** Divide the class into pairs. Ask each pair to discuss the following question: *If you could fly anywhere in a helicopter, where would you fly to and why?* After a few minutes, invite the children to share their responses in a class plenary. You may wish to display the information (places) on a map/board.

Listening

- **Reported conversations:** In pairs, ask the children to discuss whether they would like to fly in a helicopter. Once they have expressed their responses to each other, invite them to report their partner's views to the rest of the class.

Group Discussion

- **Class discussion:** Initiate a discussion on the types of rescues we see around us, in real life, in films and in the news. You may wish to list these on the board. This may be useful for the activity task (see Copymaster) in which common themes and attributes will be identified.

- **Group discussion:** Look again at the image and ask the children to suggest where the helicopter may be going and what the journey may entail. This may be described from the point of view of the pilot or of the injured person on the stretcher.

Drama

- **News reports:** In small groups of three or four, ask the children to prepare, rehearse and perform a scene in which a television newsreader announces news of the air rescue and hands over to a reporter who is on location, with eyewitnesses/pilots to interview.

Extension

- **Pilots needed!:** Working in pairs or small groups, ask the children to discuss and write down some of the qualities needed in an air rescue pilot or crew-member. What sort of person succeeds in this type of job? Each pair/grouping lists some key words and then feeds backs to the class (e.g. *brave, fit, calm under pressure, caring, strong*). You may then want them to design a short radio advertisement aimed at recruiting more pilots.

KEEP SAFE!

Working with a partner, imagine you are making a short television report to show holidaymakers and ramblers how to keep safe when walking along coastal paths.

To begin, add some more suggestions to this checklist.

- Keep away from the cliff edge.
- Keep to established footpaths.

- Don't run!
- Check weather forecasts.

_____   _____

_____   _____

Now think about how your report will look and sound. Write a short script and set it out like a playscript. Learn the words and present your report to the class.

_____

_____

_____

_____

_____

_____

_____

_____

_____

TEACHER'S NOTES

Introduction

- Load up the Mind's Eye CD-ROM. You may like to tell the children what the title of the session is before you reveal the image, or just open up the picture and watch their initial reactions to it.

- With the whole image in view, share initial responses to the scene, recording any interesting observations and comments on a mind-map on the board.

Familiarisation

- Establish that this is a hot air balloon meeting or race. Ask the children: *How many balloons are in the scene? Are some of them just landing or about to take off? Could this be some sort of annual race? To where?*

- Elicit the children's prior knowledge and experience of hot air balloons. Where and when have they seen them in the sky? Have any of them flown in a hot air balloon?

Exploration

- Look at the picture once again, and this time focus on what the swans might be thinking as these strange objects float past! Come up with similes and metaphors that describe the balloons in flight, e.g. *like giant petals on the breeze*.

- Explore possible destinations for these balloons. Where might they be heading? Encourage the children to describe possible courses for the balloons to follow, picturing the journey in their mind's eye (i.e. flying over sea, mountains, lakes and forests).

International hot air balloon festival at Leeds Castle, Kent.
© nagelstock/Alamy

ACTIVITIES

Speaking

- **Talking pairs:** In pairs, the children make a list of words that could be used to describe how it might feel to be floating across the sky in a hot air balloon. Share words and phrases in a class plenary. Good examples are: *peaceful, exhilarating, relaxing, tranquil, spectacular views, lighter than air.*

- **Talk for a minute:** Invite volunteers to talk for a minute on a given topic, drawn from objects in the image, e.g. balloons, castles, grass, trees, clouds, swans etc.

Listening

- **Reported conversations:** In pairs, the children exchange answers to the following question: *If you could take a trip in a hot air balloon to anywhere in the world, where would you fly to, and why?* Come together after a few minutes and share answers, each person speaking on behalf of their partner.

Group Discussion

- **Class discussion:** How does a hot air balloon manage to stay in the air? How does it climb or descend? Discuss the process together, with children displaying what they know in diagrammatic form on paper, or on the board.

- **Balloon debate:** Ask for 10 volunteers to each think of a famous person or well-known literary character. Explain that they are all in a balloon which is losing height and so to avoid crashing, someone must be thrown overboard! The 10 characters must write a short speech to convince the audience (rest of the class) that they are too irreplaceable to be thrown out! Listen to the speeches and vote for who stays in.

Drama

- **Group mimes:** In groups of four or five, the children prepare, rehearse and perform mimed sketches in which they are enjoying a balloon ride when suddenly something goes wrong. They are losing height and need to throw provisions overboard to climb again or they will become caught in the branches of a tree. They can only use facial expressions and body language to convey what is happening.

Extension

* **Talking to an alien:** In pairs, the children must take turns to explain to each other what a hot air balloon is, as if they were talking to someone (or something) that has never been to Earth. They will need to explain every term clearly, not assuming any prior knowledge. For example, if they say, 'The balloon is shaped like a bulb', the alien may say, 'What is a bulb?', and so on. The 'aliens' must remember to ask for clarification throughout!

Name _____   Date _____

RISING STARS BALLOON RACE

Imagine you are a radio journalist, recording live from the annual 'Rising Stars Balloon Race', set in the grounds of a beautiful castle.

Your task is to describe the event to the listeners at home, sharing what you can see, hear and feel. Remember this is radio, so you will need to describe the scene so that the listeners can visualise it with their 'mind's eye'.

Write what you will say in the space below, then learn and perform your script for the class. Ask the listeners to close their eyes before you begin speaking!

_____

_____

_____

_____

_____

_____

_____

_____

_____

_____

TEACHER'S NOTES

Introduction

- Load up the Mind's Eye CD-ROM. You may like to tell the children what the title of the session is before you reveal the image, or just open up the picture and watch their initial reactions to it.

- With the whole image in view, share initial responses. Record on the board any key words to describe the atmosphere of the scene.

Familiarisation

- Invite the children to suggest what is happening in the image. Where was it taken (which country)? How did it happen?

- Discuss bullfights and bull runs. Elicit the children's prior knowledge and experience. Is this part of a traditional 'bull run' in Spain? (The practice of running before bulls en route to the bullring is a popular 'sport' in several Spanish towns.) Have these bulls escaped from a bullfight?

Exploration

- Invite the children to consider how they would feel if a bull was running after them! Record key adjectives on a mind-map on the board, as the children picture the scene in their mind's eye (e.g. *frightened, terrified, excited, anxious, thrilled*).

- Now discuss how they would feel if they were one of the bulls in the picture. Brainstorm words and phrases again, this time from the bull's viewpoint (e.g. *angry, frustrated, frightened, hungry, confused, panic-stricken, agitated*).

A close shave in the bullring during the Pamplona Bull Run.
© Tom Bible/Alamy

ACTIVITIES

Speaking

- **Talking idioms:** Remind the children of the following idioms: '*like a bull in a china shop*' and '*take the bull by the horns*'. What do these phrases mean? Working in pairs, can the children think of other idioms? Alternatively ask them to think of similes using other animals (*as quiet as a mouse, like a bear with a sore head*).

Listening

- **Word game:** Invite two volunteers to sit opposite one another at the front of the class. The aim of the game is to call out the name of an animal that begins with the last letter of the previous one, for example; *bull* followed by *lion*, followed by *newt*, then *tiger*, and so on. Invite others to take a turn. You may also use countries of the world, boys' and girls' names, or different foods.

Group Discussion

- **Class discussion:** Explain that bullfights and bull runs have been popular sources of entertainment for Spanish people for many years. But how has entertainment changed over time? Today people flock to football matches, or pop concerts, when before they may have gone to watch a public execution! Consider different collective events, past and present, from gladiator fights to 'Proms in the Park'.

- **Class debate:** Is it right to use animals in this way? Is it cruel? What about bear-bating, fox-hunting and cock-fighting? Do they still take place? Why do we enjoy the thrill of a chase or a fight so much? Are there better forms of entertainment?

Drama

- **Hot seating:** Encourage volunteers to sit in the 'hot seat' at the front of the class and answer questions from the floor, in the role of a person in the image who is caught in the path of a stampeding bull.

- **Group play:** In groups of three or four, the children prepare, rehearse and perform a scene in which they are caught up in a bull run or bullfight where the bull escapes. The scene must be mimed, so fear/excitement should be shown in facial expressions and actions.

Extension

- **Research work:** Ask the children, in pairs, to research the traditional bull runs and bullfights of Spain. When do they take place? How many people attend? What happens to the animals at these events? What is the aim for those competing? What do others think about these practices? What is the origin of the bull run tradition? The children may use the Internet, CD-ROMs, library books, magazines and newspaper articles.

GUESS WHAT HAPPENED!

With a partner, imagine that one of you is seated in a crowd in the background of the image. What would the atmosphere be like? What can you hear?

Write a short dialogue in the space below, in which you recount the story of the stampeding bulls to your parents.

Parent: *So, what did you get up to today?   Have you had fun?* _____

Child: _____

_____

Parent: _____

_____

Child: _____

_____

Parent: _____

_____

Child: _____

_____

Parent: _____

_____

Child: _____

_____

TEACHER'S NOTES

Introduction

• Load up the Mind's Eye CD-ROM. You may like to tell the children what the title of the session is before you reveal the image, or just open up the picture and watch their initial reactions to it.

• With the whole image in view, elicit the children's initial reactions. Try to establish where and when this photograph may have been taken.

Familiarisation

• Elicit the children's prior knowledge and experience of carnivals. Can they name any famous carnivals that take place each year around the world? What sort of sights do we normally see at a street carnival? What is special about a carnival? How is it different to a procession? Where does the word come from?

• Brainstorm key words and phrases together to describe the sights and sounds of a carnival. Encourage the children to 'see' the parades in their mind's eye.

Exploration

• What do the children think the two people in the image might be saying to one another? Invite the children to suggest appropriate lines of speech.

• What is the police officer's function at the carnival? What is he doing in the image? What could go wrong at a carnival they would require a police officer?

Police officer giving directions to a participant at the Notting Hill Carnival.
© Janine Wiedel Photolibrary/Alamy

ACTIVITIES

Speaking

• **Paired work:** In pairs, ask the children to think of suitable captions that might accompany the image if it appeared in a newspaper or magazine. You may wish to offer a few sample captions on the writing board before the children set to work on their own.

• **Hot seating:** Ask for volunteers to sit at the front in the 'hot seat' and answer questions from the class, in the role of either of the two main characters in the photograph.

Listening

• **Circle game:** Ask all the children to think of an animal to base an imaginary costume on. Then invite them to stand up and move about the room, introducing themselves to each other, saying what they are dressed up as. At the end, test their listening skills by asking them to write down everyone's name and the animal they were dressed as. Can they remember who everyone was?

Group Discussion

• **Planning committee:** In groups, the children imagine they are working as a planning committee for a large street carnival in the area. They must consider: events, costumes, themes, staffing, routes and publicity. Share feedback at the end in a class plenary.

Drama

• **Duologue:** In pairs, the children pretend to be the two main characters in the photograph and prepare a short sketch in which they act out the conversation that they could be having. Share and evaluate performances at the end.

• **Group plays:** In small groups or pairs, the children imagine they are visiting a street carnival. Encourage them to use body language and facial expressions to indicate when they see interesting carnival attractions and events. You may wish to add background music to set the scene!

! Extension

• **Research:** Ask the children to find out about a particular carnival. This may be the Notting Hill Carnival in London, or perhaps a carnival in another famous city, like Rio. They may be able to access the Internet, books, magazines and CD-ROMs to locate information about the history of the carnival and the range of floats and parades that can be seen.

CARNIVAL COSTUME

Imagine you are attending a carnival. What sort of costume can you think of to dazzle the spectators?

Draw a carnival costume in the box below. You may like to think about colour, shape, materials, theme, ease of movement and cost when preparing your design.

When you have made a sketch of the costume design, present it to the class, talking through its features and general theme.

Who knows, one day you may wear one just like it!

Year 4/CHIMPANZEE

TEACHER'S NOTES

Introduction

- Load up the Mind's Eye CD-ROM. You may like to tell the children what the title of the session is before you reveal the image, or just open up the picture and watch their initial reactions to it.

- With the whole image in view, share initial responses. Record any key words on the board for future reference.

Familiarisation

- Elicit the children's prior knowledge and experience of zoos and safari parks. Which ones have they visited? What did they enjoy/dislike about them? What did the children learn about conservation/habitats and so?

- Look closely at the image. What type of mammal is this? Is it a chimpanzee? How can we tell? Discuss the children's knowledge of different primates.

Exploration

- Consider together what this chimpanzee might be thinking. Share thoughts around the class.

- Invite the children to offer words and phrases to describe the animal's natural habitat. Then consider what sort of natural resources and facilities (s)he would need in a zoo.

Chimpanzee behind bars.
© Stuart Westmoreland/Alamy

ACTIVITIES

Speaking

- **Paired work:** The children will need to work in pairs for this activity. Ask them to think up suitable captions that could be written beneath this image. A few words or a short sentence would be ideal, to sum up the chimp's feelings, or to raise the issue of keeping animals in captivity.

- **Circle game:** In a large circle, take turns to call out a word to describe a monkey's character or movements. Encourage the children to try to capture the agility and 'cheekiness' that we associate with primates of this kind. Good words are: *mischievous, inquisitive, excitable, fidgety.*

Listening

- **Story actions:** Narrate a story to the class about a visit to a zoo. As you mention certain animals that you are viewing, the children must respond with the correct actions or noises (agreed beforehand!) that one associates with each animal. They must listen out for the animal names as the story progresses.

Group Discussion

- **Class discussion:** Consider together how similar we are to chimpanzees. List, on the board, ways in which we are alike and ways in which we are different. Encourage the children to think about physical make-up, social behaviour, intellect, diet and so on.

- **Class debate:** Should animals be kept in captivity? What are the benefits of enabling children to see a range of animals in zoos and safari parks? For example, education, conservation, breeding plans and so on.

Drama

- **Hot seating:** Invite the children to take turns, either in groups or as a class, to sit in the 'hot seat' (chair at the front of the class) and respond to questions in the role of the chimp in the photograph or another animal in captivity. Encourage the children to ask good quality questions that reach for the animal's thoughts and feelings about living in a zoo.

Extension

- **Research:** Ask the children to find out more about a particular primate. They may wish to check out the following websites (and many others), or refer to books, magazines and CD-ROMs: www.primates.com   www.chimpanzoo.org
Look for 'monkey programmes' on Animal Planet on television. Once the children have found out more information, they may give a short talk to the class.

Name _____ Date _____

IF I COULD BE AN ANIMAL...

If you could be any animal in the world, what would you be?

Write down the name of your animal here.

_____

Now make some notes to explain why you have chosen this animal. You may think about where they live, any special abilities they may have and what they do when they're not sleeping!

Once you are ready, share your views with the class, remembering to support your decision with some interesting reasons.

_____

_____

_____

_____

_____

_____

_____

_____

_____

TEACHER'S NOTES

Introduction

- Load up the Mind's Eye CD-ROM. You may like to tell the children what the title of the session is before you reveal the image, or just open up the picture and watch their initial reactions to it.

- With the whole image in view, share initial responses. Encourage the children to say what they see, recording any interesting words and phrases on a mind-map on the board.

Familiarisation

- Elicit the children's prior knowledge about Egypt and the great treasures found there over the years. Discuss key words including: *tomb, sarcophagus, Pharaoh, pyramid* and so on.

- Look closely at the image. Can anyone identify animals and birds carved into the stone tomb? What is the figure holding? Is it a key? What place might the key unlock?

Exploration

- Encourage the children to consider when and where this photograph may have been taken. Could this tomb be housed within a pyramid? Who could be buried within it? A Pharaoh, perhaps, or an Egyptian prince? Share theories together.

- Invite the children to offer words and phrases to describe the king that might be buried within the sarcophagus, e.g. *grand, regal, majestic, important, powerful, leader, wealthy.*

Egyptian mummy shown as a Polaroid transfer image.
© Rob Bartee/Alamy

ACTIVITIES

Speaking

- **Talking pairs:** In pairs, the children share what they know about Egyptology. Ask them to write down any key facts, names or places on a mind-map of their own. After they have shared their ideas and experiences, invite feedback to the class. Remind the children of museums they may have visited, films seen, books read and so on.

- **Talking words:** In pairs again, ask the children to write down the word SARCOPHAGUS in large letters on a blank sheet of paper. They must then see how many words they can make using the same letters (anagrams).

Listening

- **Circle game:** Seat the class in a large circle. Explain that this photograph could have been taken by a tourist on an adventure holiday to Egypt. Then ask the children to take turns to answer the following question: *If you could visit any place for an adventure holiday, where would you go, and why?* Once you have been round the circle, test listening skills by seeing if the children can remember where others wanted to visit, and why.

Group Discussion

- **Class discussion:** In a circle, discuss mummification. What do the children know about it? Can anyone describe the process? Initiate a discussion, either as a class or in groups, in which you consider the question: *Why did the ancient Egyptians bury their dead in such an elaborate way?*

- **Narrated story:** Begin improvising a story narration, involving a holiday to Egypt. 'Pass' the story around the class, each pupil contributing a line to continue the story and build the setting. Where do the characters visit? What happens there? Could they disturb an ancient Egyptian curse?

Drama

- **Group plays:** In groups of about four or five, the children prepare, rehearse and perform a short play in which a group of friends visit a pyramid together whilst on a (school) trip. Suddenly, the great door to the pyramid slides shut and they are plunged into darkness. What happens next?

Extension

- **Group designs:** In pairs, or working individually, the children set to work designing a great tomb for an ancient Pharaoh. They will need to consider the design of the pyramid, and then the sarcophagus itself. Encourage them to think about shape, colour, materials and, most importantly, what they will include in the tomb (for the Pharaoh to take with them into the afterlife). Each pair must present their design.

Name _____ Date _____

AROUND THE WORLD

Imagine you are a reporter for a children's TV travel show. Based on what you know, and have learned in this session, write a short script on Egypt, describing the tombs and pyramids you have seen on your travels this week.

Try to describe the sounds and smells of the place, as well as the sights, so that viewers can imagine they are there with you!

_____

_____

_____

_____

_____

_____

_____

_____

_____

_____

_____

TEACHER'S NOTES

Introduction

- Load up the Mind's Eye CD-ROM. You may like to tell the children what the title of the session is before you reveal the image, or just open up the picture and watch their initial reactions to it.

- With the whole image in view, elicit the children's initial reactions. Collate ideas on the board to suggest when and where the picture may have been taken.

Familiarisation

- Elicit the children's prior knowledge of evacuees. Write the word 'evacuation' on the board and discuss it. Why were children evacuated during the war? Discuss these words: *blitz, Homefront, raids, blackouts* and *billeting*.

- Study the image more closely. Look at the condition of the buildings. What sorts of buildings were they before they were hit? Was this a town centre perhaps? Look at the children: how old are they? What are their clothes like? How can we tell this was taken some years ago?

Exploration

- Look at the faces of the children: they are smiling and laughing, so are they happy? What thoughts might be inside their heads as they leave the city? Record key words and phrases on the board.

- Invite the children to suggest words and phrases that describe the appearance and atmosphere of this place. Record the words on the board on a mind-map entitled 'Blitz'.

School children at the Ernest Reuter Platz, Charlottenburg, Berlin, May 1945.
© akg-images

ACTIVITIES

Speaking

- **Hot seating:** Ask for volunteers to sit at the front in the 'hot seat' and answer questions from the class, as one of the boys or girls in the image. Questions could relate to how they feel, what they have experienced on the Homefront, where they are going, and so on.

- **Paired work:** Ask the children to work in pairs. Each pairing must study the picture carefully and look particularly at what the children are carrying. They must make a short list of the provisions they think they would be taking with them to their evacuation billets. Remind them the year may be 1939, so no computer games!

Listening

- **Reported conversations:** In pairs, the children share their own thoughts and feelings about being evacuated. Would they feel nervous about leaving home? Would they be excited? As they listen to each other's views, they must make brief notes, recording key words and phrases so that they may report their partner's feelings to the class.

Group Discussion

- **Class discussion:** What would it have felt like for the evacuees arriving in a strange, new place in the countryside? Look again at the photograph together and try to imagine how these children may have felt once they had arrived at their billeting post.

Drama

- **Freeze frame:** In groups of about nine (although other sizes will do), ask the children to try to simulate the moment in time captured by the camera. They will need to decide who is who, and get into positions, ready for someone to 'take the photograph'.

- **Group plays:** In similar groups again, this time the children sit down and prepare a script, with each child contributing a few lines as they pretend to be the group of children in the picture. What are they saying to one another? Perhaps someone has cracked a joke! Present the scene to the class.

Extension

- **Research and presentation:** Having asked the children to imagine what it might have been like for the evacuees in the earlier activities, now ask them to research what it was *really* like for the children as they left their homes for new communities in the country. Using the Internet, books, magazines and CD-ROMs, the pupils should prepare presentations on life for the evacuees of 1939. A good website to look at is: www.thekeepinggallery.co.uk.

EVACUATION PLAN

When the government first announced that children were to be evacuated to the country, many parents would have been reluctant to let them go.

Prepare a short radio presentation to convince worried parents that evacuation is the only way of keeping their children safe during the war.

Think about:

- the dangers of staying in the city
- the fun their children will have making new friends
- the teachers and Billeting Officers who will look after them
- the lovely families they will be staying with.

Write the script for your radio broadcast below and then perform it to your class.

_____

_____

_____

_____

_____

_____

_____

_____

_____

_____

TEACHER'S NOTES

Introduction

- Load up the Mind's Eye CD-ROM. You may like to tell the children what the title of the session is before you reveal the image, or just open up the picture and watch their initial reactions to it.

- With the whole image in view, discuss the children's initial reactions. Where could this be located? What is it made of? How is it formed?

Familiarisation

- Elicit the children's prior knowledge and experience of icebergs and arctic lands. Where have they seen such sights before? In books and films ('Titanic', etc.). Discuss the difference between the Arctic and Antarctica.

- Brainstorm key words and phrases to describe the children's initial responses. Discuss *ice, frozen land, icy seas, melting snow, plateau, ice cap* and so on.

Exploration

- Discuss how this iceberg may look from other angles. What it is like on top, from above, behind and from the water below? How large could it be? Encourage the children to see the iceberg in their mind's eye. Discuss how it could have become this shape.

- Encourage the children to consider metaphors that this image could represent, i.e. interesting objects that this iceberg could be (*a giant's Lego block, giant steps, a brick from a giant igloo, a stage from an ice theatre*).

Large iceberg floating in Antarctic Sound (Antarctic Peninsula).
© Stock Connection/Alamy

ACTIVITIES

Speaking

- **Paired work:** In pairs, the children make lists of as many words as they can think of that begin with 'ice' (*ice cream, ice hockey, ice cube*). Share these in a final plenary.

- **Word tennis:** Ask for two volunteers to sit opposite one another at the front of the class and play a game in which one player 'serves' by calling out the name of a country or city located in a cold part of the world (e.g. *Alaska, Greenland*). The other player 'returns' with a new place, and so on until someone falters. You may repeat the game, this time using hot countries.

Listening

- **Narrated story:** Seated in a circle, invite the class to narrate an improvised story in which a group of explorers journey to the South Pole. You may wish to begin the story and then 'pass it around' with each child contributing one line each time. Ask the children to describe the story setting as vividly as they can.

Group Discussion

- **Class discussion:** Chair a class discussion in which you consider why such places are so hostile to Man. Why are they such difficult places to explore? (Useful preparation for 'Extension' activity below).

- **Class brainstorming:** Again as a class, brainstorm any words or phrases that capture the mood of the image, e.g. *threatening, majestic, solid, hostile*.

Drama

- **Group plays:** Divide the class into groups of about three or four. Invite each group to prepare, rehearse and perform a short play in which a group of explorers find themselves lost in a frozen wasteland. The wind is picking up and a snow blizzard is beginning to threaten their lives. What will they do? Encourage the children to make use of body language and facial expression as well as words to convey the fear they may feel.

Extension

- **Research:** Ask the children, in pairs or small groups, to find out more about the kind of wildlife that can survive in such hostile environments. Why can they live in such an environment? How have the animals evolved? They may use books, magazines, encyclopaedias, CD-ROMs and websites. Once they have found some facts, invite them to feed back to the class in short presentations.

TO BOLDLY GO...

Would you like to be an explorer? Write down an exciting place you would like to travel to and think about what it is about the location that appeals to you.

Think about:

- the landscape
- the climate
- sights and sounds you might encounter
- why this place appeals to you.

_____

_____

_____

_____

_____

_____

_____

_____

_____

_____

Once you have thought of a destination, share your thoughts and ideas with the class in a short presentation.

TEACHER'S NOTES

Introduction

- Load up the Mind's Eye CD-ROM. You may like to tell the children what the title of the session is before you reveal the image, or just open up the picture and watch their initial reactions to it.

- With the whole image in view, share initial responses. Record any key words on the board as the children 'say what they see'.

Familiarisation

- Discuss the children's prior knowledge and experience of mines like this one. Has anyone visited a mine, either a disused or a fully functioning one? Where was it located – in this country or overseas? What was mined?

- Look closely at the image together and focus on the lighting. How can the miners see to work? Is the light in the picture natural or electric?

Exploration

- Ask the children to consider where this shaft may lead to. Where does the railway track run to? Is there a light up ahead? What could be round the corner? Can the children see the shaft in their mind's eye?

- Consider together what it must be like to work underground. Brainstorm, using a mind-map on the board, key words and phrases that accurately describe conditions in a shaft like the one in the photograph.

A tunneller in the access tunnel on the Lesotho Highlands Water Project.
© qaphotos.com/Alamy

ACTIVITIES

Speaking

- **Paired work:** In pairs, the children imagine they are miners working underground more than 50 years ago. If they were trapped underground for all that time, what differences would they find when they finally returned to the surface? Think about buildings, transport, communications and so on. Share ideas in a final plenary.

- **Group brainstorm:** In groups of three or four, ask the children to list as many materials as they can think of that are extracted from beneath the Earth's surface. Examples include *gold, coal* and *diamonds*. Share answers at the end, electing a spokesperson for each group.

Listening

- **Hot seating:** In pairs, the children take turns to play the role of the miner in the foreground, while their partner asks them questions about life in the mine. They must listen carefully to each response, so that in a final plenary the children can report back what the other said in answer to the questions asked. You may wish to prescribe set questions.

Group Discussion

- **Shared story:** As a class, sit in a circle and jointly narrate an improvised story based on a mineshaft with a difference: the miners are tunnelling deep into the earth to places never explored before. What will they find?

- **Class debate:** Consider together the question: *If all forms of mining were to be abolished bar one, which natural resource would be the one we should keep mining for?* Which mined material is the most important to us? Then consider the questions: *What will happen when mined resources run out? Will we have to find alternatives?*

Drama

- **Paired dialogue:** In pairs or in small groups, the children consider what this man may be shouting to the other miners further up the shaft. After a few moments, share lines, re-enacting the scene at the front of the class.

Extension

- **Group plays:** In small groups, invite the children to act out a short scene in which they are miners working underground. You may wish to introduce some sort of crisis that requires action, e.g. the lights go out, rocks fall, or someone is injured.

Name _____   Date _____

JOB VACANCY

Find a partner. One person plays an interviewer and the other plays the part of an applicant for a job at a mine. Think carefully about the sort of skills needed to be a miner. Will this person be right for the job?

Write some questions and answers as a playscript in the space below.

Learn your words and perform the sketch to the class.

Interviewer: _____

Applicant: _____

_____

Interviewer: _____

_____

Applicant: _____

_____

Interviewer: _____

_____

Applicant: _____

_____

Interviewer: _____

_____

Applicant: _____

_____

TEACHER'S NOTES

Introduction

- Load up the Mind's Eye CD-ROM. You may like to tell the children what the title of the session is before you reveal the image, or just open up the picture and watch their initial reactions to it.

- With the whole image in view, share initial responses. Record any key words on the board for future reference.

Familiarisation

- Draw out the children's prior knowledge and experience of such buildings. Discuss key words like *mosque, temple, church, cathedral, chapel, synagogue, basilica* and *shrine.*

- Discuss what the purpose of this building might be. Where in the world might it be located? Which particular world religion might we associate with this type of building?

Exploration

- Ask the children to offer words and phrases to describe the appearance of this building. Record these on a mind-map on the board. Good examples are: *grand, peaceful, dignified, glorious, precious, cherished.*

- Invite the children to think about the interior of the building. What might it look/sound like inside? Can they think of more words to capture the atmosphere inside, using their mind's eye?

Early morning at Badshahi Mosque, Lahore, Pakistan.
© david samger photography/ Alamy

ACTIVITIES

Speaking

- **Paired work:** In pairs, ask the children to think about the building's design. What other interesting shaped buildings have they seen? Ask them to list/draw different shaped buildings that they know. They should name each one, to show it is authentic! Good examples include: *Sydney Opera House, Tower of London, Lloyds Building, St Paul's Cathedral, Le Pompidou Centre, Pyramids.*

- **Word tennis:** Ask for two volunteers to sit opposite one another at the front of the class and play a game in which one player 'serves' by calling out an example of a building material (e.g. *wood, stone, brick, steel, marble*). The other player 'returns' with a different one, and so on until someone falters through hesitation or repetition.

Listening

- **Drawing game:** In small groups, one person describes the appearance of a building orally, and the other(s) have to draw it, listening carefully to the instructions. They must not name the type of building it is until the end when they see if the other children's drawings resemble what the speaker had in mind!

Group Discussion

- **Class discussion:** What sort of building do we see when we think of England? A castle, perhaps? Buckingham Palace? Initiate a discussion in which you consider buildings that we might associate with countries around the world. For example: *pyramids/Egypt; wooden chalets/Switzerland; chateaux/France.*

- **Class debate:** Why are cathedrals and other religious buildings often very grand in appearance? Who are they for? Are these buildings more important than any other? Why do modern cathedrals, churches, synagogues and temples always seem less ornate than older ones? Should we make more of an effort now, like we used to do?

Drama

- **Duologues:** In pairs, the children prepare, rehearse and perform a scene in which they pretend to be the two people in the photograph. In a short dialogue, they discuss where they are going, who they are meeting and why.

Extension

- **Research and presentation:** Invite the children to find out more about a particular type of religious building. They may refer back to their earlier discussions of such buildings, choose one and then use the Internet, books, magazines and CD-ROMs to research it further. Questions to guide their research could include: *Who worships there? When was it built? How many worshippers attend? How often are services held?*

DESIGN YOUR OWN!

Imagine you are an architect designing a brand new place of worship for a particular religious community. The new building will house regular services, meetings and celebrations.

What materials will you use? Bricks and stones or marble and gold?

Make a sketch of your building in the space below, then draw a careful copy on a larger sheet of paper. Present your design to the class, describing its features and giving reasons for the choices you have made.

TEACHER'S NOTES

Introduction

- Load up the Mind's Eye CD-ROM. You may like to tell the children what the title of the session is before you reveal the image, or just open up the picture and watch their initial reactions to it.

- With the whole image in view, elicit the children's initial reactions. Establish that it is a grand building of some sort, photographed at night from the ground looking up, with fairy lights in a nearby tree.

Familiarisation

- Consider together where this building may be located. What sort of building could it be? What is its purpose? Record ideas on the board and discuss.

- Elicit the children's prior knowledge and experience of grand buildings such as this one. Do they recognise the architecture here? Is it similar to anything they have seen before, such as a church, cathedral, abbey, city hall, royal palace, Palace of Westminster?

Exploration

- What might this building be like inside, given its grand exterior? Ask the children to describe how the interior might look, recording key features on the board, e.g. *chandeliers, red carpets, oil paintings, archways*.

- Brainstorm what the atmosphere might be like inside the building. Record key words on a mind-map.

Ringstrasse Christmas market, Vienna, Austria.
© allOver Photography/Alamy

ACTIVITIES

Speaking

- **Paired conversations:** Working in pairs, ask the children to consider the grandest buildings they have visited or seen. Encourage them to swap stories about places they have been to. Then, in a class plenary, invite them to share their experiences, speaking for themselves, or on behalf of their partners.

- **Word tennis:** Ask for two volunteers to sit opposite one another at the front of the class and play a game in which one player 'serves' by calling out an example of a grand building (e.g. *monastery, palace, abbey, theatre, cathedral*). The other player 'returns' with a new building, and so on until someone falters, either by repeating a building already mentioned or by hesitating for too long.

Listening

- **Reported conversations:** Ask the children to consider the following question: *If you could live in any type of building, what sort would you choose, and why?* Discuss this in pairs and then invite the children to report back to the class, on their partner's behalf, or for themselves.

Group Discussion

- **Class discussion:** The building in the photograph looks a little like Hogwarts School from the 'Harry Potter' stories. Would the children like to attend a school like this? Would they find the building daunting, or would they enjoy exploring all its corridors and (moving) stairways! Discuss the kinds of school buildings they would most like to have lessons in.

- **Group talk:** In groups, ask the children to create a new design for a royal palace. Provide each group with a large sheet of paper and some pens/pencils. A consensus must be reached as they plan the design of their building, and this will require good listening and negotiating skills! Invite each group to present their work to the class at the end.

Drama

- **Group drama:** In groups of about three or four, the children prepare a scene in which they pretend they are boarders in a boarding school. They are in their dormitory, when they plan a midnight expedition up to the clock-tower. What will they find? Will they make it without being caught? Complete the scene.

Extension

- **Group stories:** In groups or as a class, invite the children to narrate an improvised story centred around the building in the photograph. Ideas for a plot/theme could be: a royal celebration that goes wrong, a haunted palace, a new year's party in a boarding school, a late night meeting in Parliament.

Name _____ Date _____

WELCOME TO THE ROYAL HOTEL

Imagine you are the manager of a large, beautiful hotel, set in an old monastery. You need to make a television advertisement to promote the hotel.

With a friend, write a script for the advertisement. Once you have thought of some lines, learn them and perform the advertisement for the class.

You will need to think about:

- the hotel's fabulous facilities
- the history of the great building
- recommendations by former guest
- prices per room and special offers.

_____

_____

_____

_____

_____

_____

_____

_____

_____

_____

TEACHER'S NOTES

Introduction

• Load up the Mind's Eye CD-ROM. You may like to tell the children what the title of the session is before you reveal the image, or just open up the picture and watch their initial reactions to it.

• With the whole image in view, discuss the children's initial reactions. Could this be real? Why would someone be somersaulting in this way?

Familiarisation

• Look closely at the image and invite the children to suggest where this may be taking place. Look at the floor, walls, furniture, pianist's attire. Is this on stage?

• Invite the children to offer theories as to why, and how, this man is somersaulting. Brainstorm these ideas on the board and decide which are the most likely. Suggestions could include: a circus act; a man who cannot play piano so entertains his audience in a different way; how someone feels nervous or excited before playing.

Exploration

• Invite the class to imagine they are in the audience, watching this piece. They have arrived at a concert, expecting a piano concerto! How do they feel now?

• Encourage the children to explore what happens next in the scene. Share ideas and record the different scenarios on the board.

Freddie Harrison, from an old performing family in Austria, at the Windmill Theatre in London, 1952.
© Black Star/Alamy

ACTIVITIES

Speaking

• **Thought-tracking:** Ask the children to suggest thoughts that might be going through this man's mind as he tumbles through the air. Share these aloud in a group or class discussion. (*'I can fly!'* or *'Bet you can't do this!'*.)

• **Word tennis:** Ask for two volunteers to sit opposite one another at the front of the class and play a game in which one player 'serves' by calling out the name of a musical instrument. The other player 'returns' with a different one, and so on until someone falters through hesitation or repetition.

Listening

• **Memory game:** Seated in a large circle, invite the class to take turns in saying which musical instrument they would play in an orchestra. Then ask for volunteers, or take turns, to see how far round the circle you can get remembering the instruments the children play.

 Group Discussion

• **Class discussion:** Think back to the exploration session when the children suggested how they might feel if they were in the audience watching this tumbling pianist! Initiate a discussion on how events sometimes don't turn out the way we expected. How do we handle this surprise? Do we laugh, cry, shout, scream, or shrug it off? Do we usually get what we planned for?

• **Paired discussion:** In pairs, ask the children to think of other interesting situations where an audience might be surprised by what they see, e.g. *an opera singer telling a joke, a vicar dancing in a pulpit, a politician singing his speech.* Come together and share feedback in a plenary.

Drama

• **Group plays:** Using some of the ideas discussed in the paired discussions above, invite the children to act out a range of surprises on stage, with artistes performing comical stunts and so on, while the audience members (the rest of the class) react to the surprise.

Extension

• **Duologues:** In pairs, the children improvise a conversation in which one person returns home from a concert at which the pianist in the photograph performed a somersault. (S)he describes the scene, and the audience's reaction to it, to a family member.

AN UNUSUAL REPORT

Imagine the person in the photo is actually in the middle of sitting a music exam. Whatever would the examiner think? Why would the student do such a thing? Perhaps he has made a mistake and decides to impress the examiner in a different way!

Imagine you are the examiner and write a report of the student's performance. Did he pass his exam? Share the report with the rest of your class.

_____

_____

_____

_____

_____

_____

_____

_____

_____

_____

_____

TEACHER'S NOTES

Introduction

- Load up the Mind's Eye CD-ROM. You may like to tell the children what the title of the session is before you reveal the image, or just open up the picture and watch their initial reactions to it.

- With the whole image in view, elicit the children's initial reactions. Collate ideas on the board to suggest where he may be.

Familiarisation

- Consider together how old this boy might be. Study his facial expression together and then brainstorm ideas about what he may be thinking. Record key words and phrases on the board, based on his mood and expression.

- Invite the children to think of suitable captions that could accompany this image and write these on the board (e.g. *bored, missing home, come and find me, lost, lonely*).

Exploration

- Initiate a short discussion about how we often need somewhere to just think. Do the children have places at home, in the house/garden, where they can find peace and quiet to sit and ponder? Do they like spending time alone sometimes? Share different 'thinking places'.

- Explore possible scenarios for how this boy came to be here. Some examples are: *playing hide and seek, missing home on a school trip to the beach, shipwrecked, can't join in friends' beach games, homeless.*

Boy in rock crevice.
© Dennis Felix/Taxi/Getty Images

ACTIVITIES

Speaking

- **Paired conversations:** The children work in pairs. One person plays the part of the boy in the image, the other is a boy/girl seated opposite them. Together they have a conversation in which the boy shares his thoughts (based on the thought-tracking work above).

- **Hot seating:** Ask for volunteers to sit at the front in the 'hot seat' and answer questions from the class, in the role of the boy in the image. Questions could be concerned with why he is there, for how long, what he is thinking, why he looks sad and so on.

Listening

- **Simon says:** Ask the children to sit in a circle, or to find individual space around the room. They must begin in the same position as the boy in the image. Then call out a series of instructions that they must follow (e.g. *raise left arm, close right eye, open mouth, move left leg*). The children must only follow your instructions if they begin with 'Simon says…'.

Group Discussion

- **Class talk (1):** Begin a class discussion on how we all need peace and quiet from time to time. Do the children ever need to be alone? Are there times when all of us crave some peace? Should we respect others' need for privacy?

- **Class talk (2):** Initiate another discussion in which you address the importance of noticing when a friend is unhappy. Should we look out more for one another? If someone in the class looks lonely and miserable, what should we do about it? What would you say to the boy in the picture if you saw him sitting there?

Drama

- **Group drama:** In groups of about three or four, the children prepare a scene in which they reveal what the boy is looking at. One person sits down as the boy, while the others mime a scene in which they are playing and having fun, but not allowing the boy to join in. We hear the boy speak his thoughts.

Extension

- **Group drama/story:** In groups of five or six, ask the children to prepare a short scene in which they are shipwrecked on a desert island, alone, without any adults. Some miss home and are worried about what will happen to them, while others are excited about the adventures they will have. Complete the scene. You may wish for one or two members of the group to act as narrators.

Name _____   Date _____

Work with a partner. One person imagines they are in the playground when they see a child sitting alone, looking glum. They approach the child and ask if they can help to cheer them up.

Your task is to perform this scene for the rest of the class. First of all, plan what you will say, then learn your lines and think about your body language and facial expressions as you act out the scene.

Child 1: _____

_____

Child 2: _____

_____

Child 1: _____

_____

Child 2: _____

_____

Child 1: _____

_____

Child 2: _____

_____

TEACHER'S NOTES

Introduction

- Load up the Mind's Eye CD-ROM. You may like to tell the children what the title of the session is before you reveal the image, or just open up the picture and watch their initial reactions to it.

- With the whole image in view, elicit the children's initial reactions. Record the first words that come into the children's minds on a mind-map on the board.

Familiarisation

- Elicit the children's prior knowledge and experience of skiing. Have they watched it on television? Has anyone been skiing? How difficult was it? Did they fall over? How difficult do they think it is to perform ski jumps? Do they think skiing is a new sport?

- Study the image more closely. Can anyone work out where the skier is, in relation to the ground? Is that a mountain behind the skier, or a cloudy sky? Is that a flag on the left? Are there really lights coming from the skis or are they the sun's reflections?

Exploration

- Explore together the feeling of performing such a jump. How must it feel to be floating through the air in such a way? Share, and record, any interesting words and phrases that the children suggest.

- Where could you find a good slope to ski down? Can the children think of any interesting places they could ski? Some examples are: *down a pyramid, on the moon, on the roof of a football stadium.*

Still from film 'Fire, Ice and Dynamite'.
© ALBUM/ALBUM/akg-images

ACTIVITIES

Speaking

- **Paired work:** In pairs, ask the children to compile a list of similes that could be used to describe the feeling of floating through air in a ski jump. For example: *as light as a feather, rising like steam, soaring like the wind.*

- **Group work:** In small groups, the children make a list of words and phrases to describe the exhilarating feeling of skiing downhill very fast (*feeling free, lots of energy, electrifying, strong, like a bullet*). Elect a spokesperson for each group and share feedback.

 Listening

- **Circle game:** Seated in a large circle together, invite the children to take turns around the circle calling out the name of a Winter Olympic sport. When someone hesitates or repeats a sport that has already been mentioned, they must sit out. Repeat the game with summer Olympic sports.

👁 Group Discussion

- **Class discussion:** Look at the image again together, focusing this time on the equipment the skier is using. Discuss what one would need to be able to go skiing. Make a list on the board. Then, for fun, see if the children can come up with alternatives that could be used for each item, e.g. poles/rolled up umbrellas, skis /planks of wood, boots/Wellingtons, and so on!

🎭 Drama

- **Group plays:** In pairs or small groups, the children prepare a short advertisement (for radio or television) for a ski holiday company, as they try to persuade potential holidaymakers to book a skiing trip with them.

- **Hot seating:** Ask for volunteers to take the 'hot seat' at the front of the class and field questions in the character of the skier in the image. Questions could refer to how they feel, how long they have been skiing, what their fears and hopes are and so on.

Extension

- **Geography talk:** In small groups, or individually, ask the children to find out more about where people ski around the world. They may use the Internet, atlases, holiday brochures and CD-ROMs. If you have access to a world map, each group may present their information by displaying the locations on the map, naming each one.

Name _____ Date _____

I'M FRIGHTENED!

With a partner, imagine you are both on a skiing holiday. One of you has skied many times before; the other has never been on a pair of skies and feels very nervous! This person suffers from vertigo (a fear of heights) as well!

Write down a few lines for each of you to perform, in which the confident skier tries to reassure the beginner that everything will be okay.

Beginner: _____

_____

Skier: _____

_____

Beginner: _____

_____

Skier: _____

_____

Beginner: _____

_____

Skier: _____

_____

Beginner: _____

_____

Year 4/SNOWY TRACK

TEACHER'S NOTES

Introduction

- Load up the Mind's Eye CD-ROM. You may like to tell the children what the title of the session is before you reveal the image, or just open up the picture and watch their initial reactions to it.

- With the whole image in view, elicit the children's first reactions to the picture and record key responses on the board.

Familiarisation

- Discuss driving in snowy conditions. Brainstorm some key words and phrases to describe the elements, such as *treacherous, bleak, icy, slippery, dangerous, lonely*.

- Elicit the children's previous experience of travelling in dangerous weather conditions. Share stories together.

Exploration

- Share theories about where this vehicle could be heading/leaving. Suggest scenarios or stories to explain why the car is there.

- Describe the land that may lie ahead/behind/to the sides. Brainstorm key words and phrases to describe the landscape (e.g. *barren, hostile, harsh, white-out*).

Jeep driving on a slippery road in winter in the highlands of Iceland.
© Nordicphotos/Alamy

ACTIVITIES

Speaking

- **Telephone conversations:** Ask the children to work in pairs, sitting back to back. The children role-play a telephone conversation in which one person is the driver of the vehicle in the picture. The car has broken down and they are calling the other person for help. The problem is: can they describe where they are located?

- **Brainstorming:** As a class, share and record similes and metaphors to describe the snowy scene in the picture. You may wish to begin with: *smooth like icing on a cake, as plain as a blank sheet of paper, snow soft as silk, ice hard as metal.*

Listening

- **Memory game:** Seat the class in a circle. Take turns reciting the following line and then adding a new animal or land feature at the end: *At Christmas I went on a snow safari and I saw...* . Before inserting a new item of their own, each person must try to remember all those that have gone before! (Examples include: *polar bear, penguin, glacier, iceberg.*)

Group Discussion

- **Class discussion:** Hold a class discussion in which you consider the most barren or remote places on Earth. List them on the board. Good examples are *the Sahara desert, Australian outback, Antarctica*. Then invite the children to think of key words and phrases that accurately capture the atmosphere of each.

Drama

- **Paired drama:** Ask the children to work in pairs. One person is lost and asks the other for directions. They could be located in a strange, remote place, or in a local area, using landmarks and routes they know.

- **Group plays:** In groups of about three or four, the children act out a scene in which they are enjoying a car journey together, driving across a remote plain. Suddenly the car breaks down – what will they do next?

Extension

- **Weather forecast:** In groups or individually, ask the children to prepare, rehearse and perform an imaginary weather forecast in which they give a warning to drivers about treacherous roads and difficult driving conditions. They must inform them where the worst areas are and how to keep safe on the roads.

LONELIEST PLACE ON EARTH

Think back to the remote places you discussed earlier. Where do you think would be the most frightening place to be left alone?

Write a few words to describe this place in the space below. Think carefully about how the place looks, sounds and feels.

_____

_____

_____

_____

Now see if you can put some of these words and phrases into a poem about your chosen land. Try to capture the sense of loneliness and helplessness that you might feel in this strange place.

Learn the poem and perform it to your class.

TEACHER'S NOTES

Introduction

- Load up the Mind's Eye CD-ROM. You may like to tell the children what the title of the session is before you reveal the image, or just open up the picture and watch their initial reactions to it.

- With the whole image in view, establish that the picture shows a spiral staircase, but are we looking up or down? Who, or what, might be producing the shadows? How many steps can you see?

Familiarisation

- Elicit the children's knowledge and experience of staircases of this kind. Where are they usually found? Have the children seen them in buildings, either in real life or in films?

- Invite the children to describe how this image makes them feel. Can they sense a mood, or atmosphere here? If the image seems ghostly, why is this? Could that really be a witch's hat in the shadows or are our imaginations working overtime?

Exploration

- Encourage the children to explore possible locations for this particular staircase. Where could it be leading us? How old could this building be? Are there any clues as to which country it is in?

- Invite the children to take turns to suggest whose shadow this is, and where they may be going. Could that be some sort of animal, perhaps a pet, following on behind?

View from beneath a spiral staircase.
© ACE STOCK LIMITED/Alamy

ACTIVITIES

Speaking

- **Group work:** Seat the class in a circle. Take turns to narrate a ghost story based on the images in the picture. Each person contributes a line each time to progress the story. Encourage the children to make special use of their voices, manipulating their tone and expression to make the story sound more dramatic.

Listening

- **Sound effects:** In pairs, ask the children to prepare a very short piece of drama in which they provide the sound effects that might accompany this image. They will need to think particularly about creating echoes of footsteps and voices.

- **Question and answer:** Divide the class into two equal lines and stand them opposite each other, with each child facing a partner on the other side. One side must take it in turns to ask a question that they would like answering about the image (e.g. where, who, why, how sort of questions). The partner opposite must provide an answer each time!

 Group Discussion

- **Discussion:** Divide the class into smaller discussion groups of about four or five. Ask each group to spend five minutes considering who might be standing at the foot of the staircase, looking up, sharing our view. Are they waiting for someone? Are they hiding? After five minutes has passed, invite each group to share their ideas.

Drama

- **Duologue:** Ask the children to get into pairs to perform a role-play in which two friends are chatting. One friend is keen to visit an old, deserted tower located in the woods, near their home. The other thinks it could be too spooky and needs persuading! What happens when they get there?

- **Group drama:** In small groups, the children pretend they are part of a film crew, making a documentary about haunted buildings across the country. In this week's live episode they are at a strange and spooky look-out tower: – and someone, or something is coming down the stairs towards them. What happens next? (See activity sheet.)

Extension

- **Group drama/story:** Invite the children to imagine that this staircase is not in a tower, but rather it begins at ground level and stretches deeper and deeper underground. Where might it lead to? For what purpose might it have been built? And, just who is coming down the stairs?

'GHOSTS' ON CHANNEL 7

As part of a new television series that investigates haunted buildings, a team of presenters have camped out in an old look-out tower. After hours of uneventful filming, suddenly a shadow appears on the staircase…

Write the script for this episode from the series 'Ghosts' and then perform it with your friends.

_____

_____

_____

_____

_____

_____

_____

_____

_____

_____

_____

_____

_____

TEACHER'S NOTES

Introduction

- Load up the Mind's Eye CD-ROM. You may like to tell the children what the title of the session is before you reveal the image, or just open up the picture and watch their initial reactions to it.

- With the whole image in view, share initial responses, recording any key words and phrases on a mind-map.

Familiarisation

- Elicit the children's prior knowledge and experience of stone circles of this kind. Where have they seen them before? How old are they? What is their purpose?

- Looking closely at the picture, discuss where and when this may have been taken. Look for clues in the grass (rural plain – countryside) and the colour of the sky (evening sun).

Exploration

- Discuss together the mood and atmosphere of the stone circle in the photograph, picturing the landscape in your mind's eye. Brainstorm any key words and phrases, for example; *ominous, eerie, spiritual, lonely, peaceful, calm.*

- Consider the question: *If these weren't stones, what could they be?* This is a simple way of introducing a metaphorical view of stones as *candles on a cake, Hong Kong skyline, tent pegs, rows of dominoes.*

Callanish Standing Stones, Island of Lewis, Outer Hebrides.
© imagestock.com/Alamy

ACTIVITIES

Speaking

- **Paired discussions:** In pairs, ask the children to think of, and write down, words that can be used to describe the appearance and feel of the stones. Good examples are; *coarse, mossy, blunt, ancient, eroded, majestic, grand, solid.* Share these in a final plenary and collate on the board.

- **Duologue:** In pairs, the children role-play the parts of two experts in the field of standing stones; historians with very different theories on why and when the stones were erected. They discuss their views and see if they can agree! You may wish to give them some theories, for example; *used for religious sacrifices, a communal shelter, a meeting place, a monument, part of a bigger stadium, a fighting ring, a theatre.*

Listening

- **Shared responses:** Propose the following question: *If the stones could listen, what sounds would they hear?* Share ideas and responses together, or in pairs. Sounds might include: *birds, distant traffic, wind, rain, thunder, aeroplanes.*

Group Discussion

- **Class discussion:** Those who built this stone circle many years ago must have felt justifiably proud of their efforts! Propose the question: *What has Man built today for which he can feel equally proud?* Think of some modern man-made structures that will make future generations question how we managed to build them with the technology of the day. You could start with *the Eiffel Tower, Golden Gate Bridge, Sydney Opera House, Empire State Building, CN Tower.*

Drama

- **Group drama:** In small groups, the children prepare, rehearse and perform a short play in which they are a group of friends who discover a forgotten stone circle. As they stand at its centre, suddenly a loud clap of thunder strikes. What happens next? Share performances in class.

- **Group movement:** In groups of five or six, and in a large open space, ask the children to form a stone circle, like the one in the image. Explain that you are going to simulate a lightning flash at which point the stones are 'struck' by lightning and come to life. How would they move? Would they stretch? How would they walk? Share group performances.

Extension

- **Research project:** Ask the children to conduct further research into famous stone circles around the world. You may wish to guide their investigations by setting a series of specific questions that might begin with: what, why, where, when, how and who.

IF THE STONES COULD TALK...

Think again about the sounds that the ancient stones would have heard if they had been listening all this time. If they could talk, what do you think they would say to one another?

Write a poem about bringing the great stones to life and describing the stories they could tell about their lives up on the moors.

Learn your poem and perform it for the class.

Morning!

Cold today, isn't it?

_____

_____

_____

_____

_____

_____

_____

_____

_____

_____

_____

_____

TEACHER'S NOTES

Introduction

- Load up the Mind's Eye CD-ROM. You may like to tell the children what the title of the session is before you reveal the image, or just open up the picture and watch their initial reactions to it.

- With the whole image in view, discuss the children's initial reactions and responses to the picture of the submarine. Look also at the number of different colours in the image.

Familiarisation

- Elicit the children's prior knowledge of submarines: where have they seen/read about them before? What are they used for? Has anyone seen/been on one themselves?

- Encourage the children to consider where in the world this could be. Where could the submarine be heading? Is it rising or diving? What time of day is this? (Look at the colours.)

Exploration

- Discuss what the atmosphere inside the submarine might be like and brainstorm some key words and phrases. Encourage the children to see the interior of the submarine with their mind's eye: e.g. *claustrophobic, cramped, metallic echoes, beeps, disciplined, tough.*

- Ask the children to consider what sort of mission this submarine might be engaged in. Could it be on a training exercise in peace-time, or is it involved in a sea battle?

USS City of Corpus Christi nuclear submarine.
© Brand X Pictures/Alamy

ACTIVITIES

Speaking

- **Paired conversations**: In pairs, ask the children to think about the sort of qualities a submariner would need to cope with life on board. Each pair writes down some key words and then shares them in a final plenary. Good examples are: *calm, methodical, self-disciplined, courageous.*

- **Circle talk**: In a circle, invite each child to think of a word to describe how the submariners must feel when they finally reach the open hatch and see the sunshine again after a long dive. They may describe their feelings, or the scene that surrounds them.

Listening

- **Reported conversations**: In pairs, ask the children to share their views on whether or not they would like to work on a submarine. Once they have expressed their responses to each other, invite them to report their partner's views to the rest of the class.

 Group Discussion

- **Class discussion**: Begin a class discussion on how much people rely on the sea. How do we use it? How do we benefit from it? List on the board the different ways in which we use and benefit from the sea. You may wish to divide the information into categories: e.g. leisure, transport, resources.

- **Group discussion**: In groups, ask the children to think about how sea battles and wars have changed over the years. How did people fight many years ago? What were their ships like? How did battles change when submarines were invented? Share feedback at the end of the session.

Drama

- **Group plays**: Divide the class into groups of about three or four pupils. Each group must act out a scene in which they are sailors on board a submarine. Provide each group with a different scenario to explore, such as: caught in a battle; problems with power; mutiny on board; setting off for the first time; coming home.

Extension

- **Research work**: Invite the children to find out more about submarines, using the Internet, library books, magazines and CD-ROMs. You may wish to guide their research through the use of key questions: e.g. *When were submarines first invented? How much does a modern submarine cost to build/run? What sorts of tasks do submariners actually do on board?*

Name _____   Date _____

THE LONG VOYAGE

With a partner, role-play a scene between a nervous new recruit to submarine life and a submariner who has been working underwater for many years.

Have a conversation in which you share feelings about what lies ahead as you prepare to dive.

Write your conversation out as a playscript, then learn your words and perform the scene to the rest of the class.

Sailor 1: _____

_____

Sailor 2: _____

_____

Sailor 1: _____

_____

Sailor 2: _____

_____

Sailor 1: _____

_____

Sailor 2: _____

_____

Sailor 1: _____

_____

TEACHER'S NOTES

Introduction

- Load up the Mind's Eye CD-ROM. You may like to tell the children what the title of the session is before you reveal the image, or just open up the picture and watch their initial reactions to it.

- With the whole image in view, elicit the children's initial reactions. Collate words and phrases on the board to sum up their first reactions.

Familiarisation

- Elicit the children's prior knowledge and experience of swimming in the sea. Where have they been for a seaside holiday? Have they swum in seas around the British Isles? Have they been elsewhere? What was the difference? Think about temperature, colour, cleanliness, marine life.

- Study the image more closely. Is that land in the distance behind the swimmers, or is it another wave? Is that a rock on the left? Who might be holding the camera? Encourage the pupils to orientate their way around the scene, constructing a wider view of the landscape in their mind's eye.

Exploration

- Look at the faces of the swimmers. Are they happy? Brainstorm words and phrases to sum up how they may be feeling, for example: *relaxed, excited, cold, tired, nervous, happy.*

- Where might the swimmers be on holiday? Invite the children to suggest scenarios for where they are, what their holiday is like, what they will do next and so on.

Woman and two children swimming in a lake.
© David Coperman/Alamy

ACTIVITIES

Speaking

- **Hot seating:** Ask for volunteers to sit at the front in the 'hot seat' and answer questions from the class, as one of the swimmers in the picture. Questions could include: *When did you learn to swim? Why are you wearing goggles? What does the sea feel like?*

- **Paired work:** Ask the children to work in pairs. Each pairing must make a list of all the creatures they can think of that may be lurking below these swimmers' feet. Share lists at the end and see who has recorded the most. Sensible suggestions only! You may like to specify where this sea could be, such as the UK, Barbados, Spain, etc.

Listening

- **Memory game:** Seat the children in a circle together. The children must take turns to recite the following line out loud, adding a sea creature of their choice at the end: *Last summer I went paddling in the sea and I saw a... .* Each child must repeat all previous creatures before they add their own!

Group Discussion

- **Class discussion:** Initiate a class discussion on keeping safe when swimming in the water. Devise a set of guidelines, to be written on the board, which should be followed by all children when at the coast, e.g. *never swim without an adult, always stay close to the shore, never swim out of your depth.*

Drama

- **Still images:** In groups of four if possible, the children enact this scene, with three swimmers and the fourth member of the family taking the photograph. Then they set about building other images that might appear as holiday snaps in the family's holiday album, such as walking on the pier, eating fish and chips, playing on a carousel, feeding seagulls, enjoying a boat ride, and so on. Share images at the end.

- **Group plays:** In similar groups again, this time the fourth person acts as the narrator of a mini-play involving the other three swimmers. As the narrator improvises a story describing a scene which may involve some sort of adventure/crisis in the water, the 'actors' must mime the story as it unfolds, adding facial expressions and so on.

Extension

- **Research and presentation:** Where are the best beaches in the world? Where are the worst? Encourage the children to research coastal resorts around the world, using atlases, holiday brochures and websites. Think of criteria first, and then in pairs or small groups, the pupils present their findings to the group. Will the UK's beaches come out on top?

Name _____   Date _____

SWIMMING IS COOL (IF YOU FOLLOW THE RULES)

You will need to work in pairs, or groups of three for this activity.

Write, rehearse and perform a short children's television broadcast, to encourage young viewers to remember some important rules before they go swimming at the seaside.

Try to think of some catchy ways of getting the message across, so that the viewers will enjoy it and also remember what you say!

Write down what you are going to say first, then learn your words and perform them as if you were on television.

_____

_____

_____

_____

_____

_____

_____

_____

_____

_____

TEACHER'S NOTES

Introduction

- Load up the Mind's Eye CD-ROM. You may like to tell the children what the title of the session is before you reveal the image, or just open up the picture and watch their initial reactions to it.

- With the whole image in view, elicit the children's first impressions, recording their words on a mind-map on the board. These may be the names of the items inside, and words associated with this image.

Familiarisation

- Ask the children to look closely at the image and see if they can memorise what is inside the briefcase. Then cover the image and ask the children, in pairs, to test each other on its contents. Can they remember all the items inside?

- Talk briefly about how this photograph was taken. Discuss that it is a scanned image from an x-ray machine, used by security officers at airports. How does it work? Why do they need it? What might it detect? Why would it be useful at an airport?

Exploration

- Look closely at the items in the briefcase again. Encourage the children to discuss the significance of each. For example; *What are the keys for? What is on the floppy disk? What could be written in the notepad?*

- Ask each child to think about one of the objects in detail and invent some interesting facts or stories about the item. Some ideas to start are: *the keys are for a flat in Monaco; the floppy disk contains top secret information.* Share stories and theories.

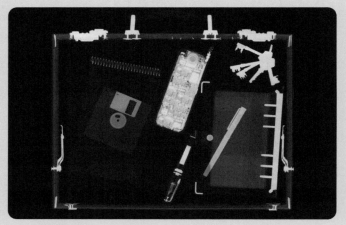

X-ray image of briefcase.
© Image Source/Alamy

ACTIVITIES

 ### Speaking

- **Word tennis:** Hold a 'tournament' in which two players face each other and take quick turns in naming an item that you might see in someone's holiday luggage bag. If a player hesitates, the other wins the game.

- **Interrogation:** In pairs, the children prepare a short scene in which one person is a special agent hunting down a spy who has stolen vital government information on a computer disk. A tip-off from customs officers leads the agent to the owner of this bag. Could this be the culprit at last? There are some tricky questions to be answered (see activity sheet for script).

Listening

- **Five questions:** In pairs, the children take turns to think of an object from the briefcase. The other partner must ascertain what the object is by asking no more than five questions. The answer to the questions may only be 'yes' or 'no'.

- **Hot seating:** Invite volunteers to take the 'hot seat' and answer questions from the floor in the role of the person who owns the briefcase. *Where is (s)he going? Why has (s)he got a disk with her? What does (s)he do for a living? Is this a business trip or a holiday?*

 ### Group Discussion

- **Discussion:** Hold a class discussion on whether or not it is right to search someone's luggage. What exactly are we looking for when we x-ray luggage at airports? What would happen if someone refused?

- **Group stories:** Working as a whole class, invite the children to take turns in narrating a line of an improvised story involving the briefcase. Perhaps the story could be about a secret agent sent on a mission.

Drama

- **Improvising with props:** Working in small groups, the children must take three items at random from the briefcase and construct a story or mini-play in which these items are in some way connected and serve a purpose of some sort.

Extension

- **Time capsule:** Propose a theory that the briefcase in the picture is a time capsule, buried for future descendants to find. If the children had to fill their own capsule, what would they put in it? Invite them to prepare a short speech explaining and defending their choice of objects.

Name _____ Date _____

DOES THIS BELONG TO YOU?

A suspicious bag has been found at a UK airport. It contains a mysterious disk, but the bag's owner refuses to tell detectives what is on it.

Working with a partner, write the script for the interrogation, beginning each time with the police officer's questions.

Officer: _____

_____

Suspect: _____

_____

Officer: _____

_____

Suspect: _____

_____

Officer: _____

_____

Suspect: _____

_____

Officer: _____

_____

Suspect: _____

_____

TEACHER'S NOTES

Introduction

- Play a short section of the audio clip and pause it. Invite the children to suggest who, or what, is producing this sound and why.

- Continue playing the clip to the end. Share the children's first impressions of the sound. Record any interesting observations on the board and establish that it is the sound of drums and chants. Key words might include: *rhythms, chants, drums, repeating pattern, African style, tribal dances.*

Familiarisation

- Ask the children to consider where this might be taking place. Share and write down their suggestions: e.g. *in a rainforest, in a tribal village, on a stage.*

- Elicit the children's prior knowledge and experience of African drumming and dancing of this kind. Has anyone seen/heard African drumming before? How did it make them feel?

Exploration

- Explore words and phrases to capture how such music affects us. Describe the emotions we feel when we hear such noises, for example: *excited, frightened, curious, fidgety, energetic, happy.* Encourage the children to take turns articulating how this music makes them feel.

- Explore together, using a mind-map on the board, what this drumming might represent, as a metaphor (what it sounds like). Begin by suggesting: *a train moving along the tracks* or *a machine in progress.* Share interesting ideas.

Audio clip
AFRICAN DRUMS (29 secs)

ACTIVITIES

Speaking

- **Talking partners:** Working in pairs, ask the children to list all the instruments they can think of from the percussion family: e.g. *cymbals, triangle, snare drum, cow bell, maracas,* and so on. Share lists at the end and see who has the most. Can the children describe them all, for those who have never heard some of them.

- **10 questions:** In pairs, one child thinks of a percussion instrument, then invites their partner to guess their instrument, by asking up to 10 questions, the answers to which may only be yes or no.

Listening

- **Clapping syllables:** In a circle, introduce the idea of syllables by clapping out some names for the children, placing stresses on each new syllable. Invite each pupil to do the same for their names.

- **Rhythm patterns:** In a circle, clap out a series of different rhythm patterns with your hands, which the children must repeat back to you, either individually, or as a class. Gradually make the rhythms more complex. Can they clap out the rhythm from the audio clip?

Group Discussion

- **Dancing around the world:** In a circle, begin a discussion on dances and customs that you find around the world. Can the children think of any interesting dances that one might associate with a particular country? Good examples are Morris dancing/England; line dancing/USA; Irish dancing/Ireland.

- **Group discussion:** Divide the class into groups of about three. Each group must begin a brief discussion on fairy tales, with a particular focus on the villains or 'baddies' that so many fairy tales seem to feature. Ask the children to consider why so many fairy tales and traditional folk tales have villains in them. Is it so that we can then have a hero? Is it because we like to see good conquering evil?

Drama

- **African tribe:** In groups of about six, the pupils prepare, rehearse and perform a short sketch in which some of them are trekking across Africa when they stumble across a tribe, dancing around a fire. We see the tribal dance in full flow, then the visitors are welcomed into the circle and taught the dance. At the end, the players discuss (in character) what the dances mean.

Extension

- **Music around the world:** In small groups or pairs, the children make a list of different forms of music from around the world. They may use a range of resources to find out their information, including the Internet, CD-ROMs and music encyclopaedias. Some examples are: *reggae/Jamaica, blues/Africa and Southern states of USA, country and western/USA, flamenco/Spain and Latin America, ska/UK.*

RAPPING FOR AFRICA

Listen to the drumming in the clip once again and think about turning it into a rap.

In groups of three or four, practise marking a slow and steady beat with your hands or with percussion instruments.

Now write a few words to go over the top of the rhythm. Your rap could be about Africa and the animals you might find there.

Write out your rap, then learn your words and perform it to the class.

Verse 1: _____

_____

_____

_____

Chorus: _____

_____

_____

_____

Verse 2: _____

_____

_____

_____

TEACHER'S NOTES

Introduction

- Play the first few seconds of the audio clip and then pause it. Invite the children to suggest what or who might be making these sounds.

- Continue to play the rest of the clip for the class, then elicit the children's first reactions to the whole clip. Share any key words and phrases on the board.

Familiarisation

- Replay the clip and then establish that this is one or more dolphins calling. Do the children recognise the sounds? Can they identify the sound of water too? (In the final few seconds there is a splashing sound.)

- Elicit the children's prior knowledge and experience of dolphins. Where and when have they seen them? Have they heard the noises they make before? Has anyone seen a dolphin in real life? How did they feel? What is the difference between a dolphin and a porpoise?

Exploration

- Invite the children to explore words and phrases that describe dolphins: their appearance, behaviour and the images and feelings they conjure up, such as *graceful, elegant, streamlined, friendly, serene, agile.*

- Replay the clip again. Can the children put the sounds they are hearing into words? Share ideas on the board. Good examples are *clicking, whistling, squealing, humming.*

Audio clip
DOLPHIN CALL (09 secs)

ACTIVITIES

 ### Speaking

- **Talking pairs:** Play the clip once again and ask the children, working in pairs, to make a list of the animals and insects that might make similar sounds, such as *crickets and grasshoppers clicking, woodpeckers knocking, monkeys squealing, birds singing* and so on. Share results in a class plenary. Encourage the children to try to simulate the sounds they mention!

- **Alliteration:** In pairs, ask the children to discuss and write down as many alliterative phrases as they can using different sea creatures and accompanying adjectives, beginning with *dancing dolphins.* Other examples include: *crawling crabs, shy sharks, jumping jellyfish, lolloping lobsters.*

 ### Listening

- **Animal sounds:** Working initially in pairs, and then performing for the class, the children act out conversations as different animals called out by the teacher. For example, if 'dogs' is called out, the pupils must bark to one another as though they were in conversation, using expression and intonation. Other animals could include: *lions, birds, gorillas, pigeons.*

 ### Group Discussion

- **Class research:** Consider together where dolphins live. Where are they found around the world? Are they an endangered species? You may like to invite the children to research dolphins before the discussion and then share their findings in class.

- **Class discussion:** Pose the following question to the class: *If you could be any creature in the sea, what would you be, and why?* Encourage the children to think for a few moments, then express their choices, supporting their decisions with reasons and explanations.

Drama

- **Talking dolphins:** In groups of about four, the children act out and translate a dolphin conversation. Two children simulate the sounds on the clip, while the others translate each noise into a line of dialogue. You may wish to replay the clip to remind the children how dolphins communicate.

Extension

- **Poems:** Individually or in pairs, the children plan, compose and then redraft their poems entitled 'Swimming with dolphins'. Brainstorm some interesting descriptive words and phrases to stimulate the class. Once the poems are written, invite the children to learn their poems and then perform them to the class.

Name _____ Date _____

DEAR HUMANS

If dolphins could talk or write, what might they say to us?

From the point of view of the dolphin, imagine you have been asked to write to humans, to tell them how important it is that they look after planet Earth. Remind humans how they should take care of the oceans or risk losing the treasures that lie within it.

Remember! Dolphins are very clever creatures, so your letter will need to be well written!

Dear Humans,

_____

_____

_____

_____

_____

_____

_____

_____

_____

_____

TEACHER'S NOTES

Introduction

- Play the first few seconds of the audio clip and then pause it. Invite the children to suggest what might be making this sound.

- Continue to play the whole clip for the class. Invite the children to guess again what is making the sound (an elephant).

Familiarisation

- Elicit the children's prior knowledge and experience of elephants. Where have they seen/heard them before? Has anyone seen an elephant in the wild/captivity? Can they describe how they felt when they saw the elephant?

- What do we associate with elephants? What do we think of when we hear the word 'elephant'? Brainstorm key words and phrases on the board, for example: *strong, sturdy, reliable, heavy, gentle giants, good memory, endangered, precious, trunks.*

Exploration

- Play the audio clip again and invite the pupils to suggest what might be causing the elephant to make this noise. Good suggestions are: *feeling threatened, angry, hungry, calling tribe, attracting a mate* etc.

- Discuss other animal noises one might hear on an elephant safari. Share and record these on the board (for use below). Some examples are: *wild cat growling, snake hissing, monkeys chattering, fireflies and crickets clicking* and so on.

Audio clip
ELEPHANT BULL (10 secs)

ACTIVITIES

Speaking

- **Alliteration:** Working in pairs, ask the children to make a list of alliterative phrases that involve jungle animals in some way, beginning with elephants, e.g. *elephants eat everything, monkeys make models, snakes sneer at snails, leopards leap over lakes* and so on.

- **Talk for a minute:** Invite volunteers to talk for a minute on a topic provided, beginning with elephants. Related topics are: *trunks, big feet, gentle giants, forgetfulness, mother nature, on safari, zoos.*

Listening

- **Memory game:** Seat the class in a circle. Invite a volunteer to begin the game by reciting the following and adding an animal of their choice: *Last year I went on an elephant safari. I didn't see any elephants but I did see...* Once the first speaker has begun, take turns reciting the sentences and remembering all the animals that went before, then adding a new one each time.

 Group Discussion

- **Class discussion:** Elephants are amongst the most respected and valued animals in the world. They capture our imagination and always inspire those who are lucky enough to get close to them in the wild. Why are elephants so appealing? Share ideas about what makes elephants so interesting.

- **Class discussion:** The phrase 'an elephant never forgets' has become well known, but from where did it originate? Why should an elephant have a better memory than, say, a giraffe, or a whale? Invite the children to share their ideas.

Drama

- **Group plays:** In small groups, the children prepare, rehearse and perform scenes which include the sound clip of the elephant's call. The children will need to invent scenarios to explain why the elephant is behaving in this way, such as being threatened by hunters, treated by vets, trained in a zoo, etc. Alternatively the children could be a group on safari who encounter an angry elephant!

Extension

- **Paired work:** In pairs, the children use a range of resources to research and answer the following question: *What are the differences between an African elephant and an Indian elephant?* Check out www.thebigzoo.com for useful information, or http://en.wikipedia.org/wiki/Elephant. Introduce the word 'pachyderm'.

Name _____ Date _____

ENDANGERED ANIMALS

When a species is threatened with extinction, we call it 'endangered'.

Working with a partner, find out more about the endangered animals of the world. You can use the Internet, CD-ROMs, books and magazines.

Write down your findings in the space below, then present your information to the class.

_____

_____

_____

_____

_____

_____

_____

_____

_____

_____

_____

Mind's Eye/Speaking & Listening   Year 4/ELEPHANT

TEACHER'S NOTES

Introduction

- Play the first few seconds of the audio clip and then pause it. Invite the children to explain what could be making this sound. Focus not only on the siren, but also on the sound of skidding tyres.

- Continue to play the whole clip for the class. Discuss the children's first impressions. Record any key words and phrases on the board. Encourage them to 'say what they hear' in this initial stage.

Familiarisation

- Replay the clip and then share ideas about what could be making this set of sounds: e.g. *a police car or ambulance vehicle swerving through traffic with siren blaring, or a criminal being chased.*

- Elicit the children's prior knowledge and experience of such emergencies. What do other drivers do when they hear this noise? Why is it often difficult to identify where the sound is coming from?

Exploration

- Where might this vehicle be racing to, and why? Invite the children to suggest reasons why the police car, or ambulance, may be racing through traffic.

- How might the pedestrians and other drivers have felt when they heard this noise, and saw the speeding vehicle(s) through the traffic? Brainstorm words and phrases on the board. These words are a good starting point: *anxious, excited, nervous, worried, confused, panic-stricken, calm.*

Audio clip
AMERICAN POLICE CAR (10 secs)

ACTIVITIES

 ### Speaking

- **Talking pairs:** In pairs, encourage the children to consider what happened next, after the sound of the siren stopped. Did the police car catch up with the criminal? Did the ambulance arrive on the scene? What did they find? Share ideas and then report back to the group.

- **City noises:** In small groups, ask the children to make a list of the sorts of noises you might hear in a city centre, beginning with the siren in the audio clip. Share lists at the end and see who has collected the most sounds. Examples include: *car horns, pelican-crossing beeps, engine noise, pedestrians shouting, van doors slamming, cage doors sliding over shop windows* etc.

 ### Listening

- **Story actions:** Seat the class in a large circle. Explain that you are going to narrate an improvised story set in a city centre, and involving a selection of the city sounds discussed earlier. Whenever you mention an item that makes a noise, such as *car, van, crossing*, the children must make the noise. See who is listening carefully and who follows the rest!

- **Listening game:** In a circle, the children take turns to answer the following question, as the others listen carefully: *If you could be a police officer, firefighter or paramedic, which would you be, and why?* At the end, the children must write down how many of each there are in the group.

 ### Group Discussion

- **Class discussion:** What must it be like to work as a police officer in a large city? Initiate a discussion on the sorts of tasks a police officer might face on the beat in a city centre and then consider the qualities (s)he might need to be successful in the role.

Drama

- **TV reporters:** In pairs or small groups, the children pretend they are television reporters/witnesses live on the scene of an accident or car chase in a city centre. They must describe what they heard, saw and felt as the sirens started wailing. Share performances at the end of the session.

Extension

- **Poems:** Individually or in pairs, the children write a poem describing the atmosphere in a city centre when a siren is heard and the drivers must all quickly move out of the way. Remind them of the key words and phrases already brainstormed and encourage them to bring the scene to life with adjectives, adverbs and abstract nouns.

Name _____ Date _____

OFFICER'S REPORT

Imagine you are the driver of the vehicle you heard in the clip. You need to decide whether you are a police officer or an ambulance driver.

When you return to your headquarters later that day, your manager asks you to give an account of what happened. Write what you might say in the space below and then read your report to the class.

Remember: you are describing the scene from the driver's point of view.

_____

_____

_____

_____

_____

_____

_____

_____

_____

_____

_____

TEACHER'S NOTES

Introduction

• Play the first few seconds of the audio clip and then pause it. Invite the children to explain what could be making this sound.

• Continue to play the whole clip for the class. Discuss the children's first impressions and record any key words and phrases on the board. Encourage them to try to name and classify the different sounds they hear, such as *a beep, hum, buzz*, etc.

Familiarisation

• Replay the clip and then share ideas about what could be making this series of hums and buzzes. Record the children's ideas on the board. Their examples may include *an alien space craft, an electronic lift, a hovering robot, a futuristic car.*

• Elicit the children's prior knowledge and experience of UFOs. What do the letters stand for? Why do we often think of UFOs as plate-shaped? Can we really know what they sound like? What is it in their design that would make them sound like this?

Exploration

• Play the audio clip again and invite the children to explore possible scenarios for this sound: are they about to be carried away on a flying saucer? Have the aliens landed? Or are the children living in the next century, travelling in a lift up to the 200th floor?

• Explore words and phrases that could be used to describe the characteristics of the sounds on the audio clip, for example, *space-age, futuristic, efficient, electronic, modern, computerised, technical.*

Audio clip
FLYING SAUCER (12 secs)

ACTIVITIES

Speaking

• **Talking pairs:** In pairs, the children choose their favourite theory about what this sound may be and then prepare a short speech explaining, in detail, why their theory is the most likely. At the end of the session, invite the class to vote for the idea they most like/believe.

• **Explanations:** In pairs, the children must take turns to describe the sound on the clip without actually recreating any of the noises. They may only use proper words to describe the sound to the other person, who must pretend they have never heard the sound before and ask questions for clarification.

Listening

• **Sound simulation:** In pairs or small groups, encourage the children to attempt to simulate the audio clip, recreating the sounds they hear with nothing but their own voices! Listen to, and evaluate, the children's attempts. Play the clip once again and assess which group sounds the most similar.

 Group Discussion

• **Class discussion:** Begin a class discussion about the type of sounds that we frequently hear today which might have sounded very strange to our ancestors. Some ideas include *telephone ringing, computer switching on off, alarm clock, helicopter.* What sort of noises can we expect to hear in years to come? Will they sound like the ones in the clip?

Drama

• **Paired mimes:** Working in pairs, ask the children to prepare a short series of actions that might accompany the sounds on the clip. Watch each mini-performance at the end, adding the sound effects each time, and then ask the children to explain what they were doing in the scene. Which was the most realistic?

• **Group drama:** In small groups, set the children the task of preparing, rehearsing and performing a short play in which they find themselves trapped on an alien ship, bound for a distant planet. The sound may open the scene: the noise of their cell being sealed and the space craft setting off. How do they feel? What will happen to them?

Extension

• **Sound engineers:** In small groups, the children prepare the sound effects that might accompany a battle in space between two flying saucers. The entire sequence needs to be recreated through sound, from the radar detectors, locating an enemy ship, to warning shots and laser beams being fired! How will the conflict end?

STRANGE NEW WORLD

Imagine you are the captain of the alien space craft that you can hear in the audio clip. You have been sailing through space for many months, when you pick up a signal on your radar system and planet Earth is revealed.

Write the conversation you might have with your officer the moment you see Earth for the first time, then perform your conversation to the class.

Captain: _____

_____

Officer: _____

_____

Captain: _____

_____

Officer: _____

_____

Captain: _____

_____

Officer: _____

_____

Year 4/HOWLING WIND

Introduction

- Play the first few seconds of the audio clip and then pause it. Invite the children to explain what could be making this sound. Write suggestions on the board.

- Continue to play the whole clip for the class. Revisit the children's first impressions, recording any key words and phrases on the board. Encourage the children to 'say what they hear' in this initial stage.

Familiarisation

- Replay the clip and then establish that this is probably the sound of the wind in some desolate place. Encourage the children to suggest where this sound might be from, such as: *the arctic, a desert, the Moon* and so on.

- Elicit the children's prior knowledge and experience of high winds. What do we call a particularly severe wind? A good suggestion is to work up from a gale to a hurricane. Has anyone experienced a gale, or even a hurricane, first hand? How did it feel?

Exploration

- Invite the children to explore words and phrases that capture the mood of the sound clip. Encourage them to see the location in their mind's eye and then to list powerful adjectives to describe its atmosphere, such as *desolate, lonely, frightening, harsh, inhospitable.*

- Play the clip once again and then invite the children to describe what the landscape in their mind actually looks like, as they hear the howling wind and picture themselves in a desolate place, for example: *'I can see flat sand stretching for miles'* or *'I am caught in a white out in the arctic'* or *'The lunar surface is rocky and grey'.*

Audio clip
EERIE HOWLING (26 secs)

ACTIVITIES

Speaking

- **Talking pairs:** In pairs, encourage the children to listen to the clip again and imagine they are involved in an expedition to a desolate place. Ask them to identify, and write down, the place they are exploring, then prepare a short conversation, in which they describe the journey so far.

- **Shared story:** Seat the class in a circle. Begin narrating a story involving a hurricane. As the story is 'passed around' the circle, each child adds a line of narration. Encourage the storytellers to use descriptive language to set the scene and paint a vivid picture.

Listening

- **Building sounds:** Play the recording once again. Invite the children, in pairs, to add extra sounds that might fit in with the clip. For example: *thunder crashing, cries for help from someone stranded, animals in distress, a lonely bird.* Replay the audio clip and share performances. Which sound effects were the most appropriate in this context?

Group Discussion

- **Class discussion:** Elicit the children's prior knowledge about how hurricanes are measured. What do they know about the phrase 'Force ten'? Discuss hurricanes around the world and the devastation they can cause. How could we protect ourselves if we were living in a location that experienced hurricanes?

Drama

- **TV reporters:** In pairs or small groups, the pupils present a news report on a hurricane that hits this country. One person will need to be the newsreader in the studio, while the other(s) will be a reporter on location and any witnesses who have been caught up in the strong winds.

- **Gale warning:** Ask the children to prepare individual presentations in which they pretend to be a weather presenter, announcing warnings of strong gales ahead. Share and evaluate performances at the end.

⚠ Extension

- **Metaphors:** Ask the children to write a poem in which they compare the wind to other strong, frightening forces, using similes and metaphors such as: *the wind picked up cars and hurled them like a giant's fist, the wind rattled around the empty houses like a pinball machine.* What do we mean by 'the eye of the storm'?

Name _____ Date _____

Human inventions can be deafening – think about car engines, machinery, rockets and even explosions – but Mother Nature can be just as loud!

Working with a partner, make a list of sounds that you might hear in the natural environment. For each sound, write one or two adjectives to describe it.

Natural sound	**Description**
Strong winds	

Now present your list to the class and describe each sound you have listed. Which would you find the most frightening? Which is the loudest?

TEACHER'S NOTES

Introduction

- Play the first few seconds of the audio clip and then pause it. Invite the children to suggest where this sound might have been recorded, from what they have heard so far.

- Continue to play the whole clip for the class. Discuss the children's first impressions and record any key words and phrases on the board. Encourage the children to identify how many different sounds they can hear.

Familiarisation

- Replay the clip and then discuss where this may have been recorded. If it is the sound of animals and insects, where are they located (*jungle, rainforest*)?

- Elicit the children's prior knowledge and experience of jungles and rainforests. Where are they located around the world? What is the climate like? What is the vegetation like?

Exploration

- Explore the types of animals that could be making these sounds and list them on the board. Starting off points are *crickets, cicadas, fireflies, parrots, macaws, monkeys* and so on.

- Encourage the children to explore words and phrases that could be used to describe the setting and atmosphere of the jungle, as they see the landscape in their mind's eye (e.g. *humid, mysterious, cluttered, overgrown, wild, hostile, threatening, lonely*).

Audio clip
JUNGLE ATMOSPHERE (04 secs)

ACTIVITIES

Speaking

- **Travelling partners:** In pairs, the children prepare a short conversation in which one is keen to explore a jungle and the other has a fear of creepy crawlies and needs persuading! Perform the scenes and share feedback.

- **Hot seating:** Invite the children take turns to sit in the 'hot seat' at the front of the classroom. Each person must answer questions in the role of a jungle explorer. Questions could search for information about the atmosphere, sights, sounds and daily rituals in the jungle.

Listening

- **Word tennis:** Encourage two volunteers at a time to sit opposite one another at the front of the class. The first player 'serves' by calling out a jungle animal. The partner 'returns' with a second animal, and so on until someone falters through hesitation or repetition.

- **Listening game:** Narrate a story about trekking in the jungle. Before you begin give everyone an animal to play. Every time you mention a particular animal, the person(s) must make the appropriate sound. They will need to listen carefully to keep up with the story!

Group Discussion

- **Class discussion:** Why is the rainforest so important to us? How is it threatened? Initiate a class discussion on deforestation and conservation issues. Elicit what the children already know about these issues, encouraging them to share their knowledge and learn new facts from one another.

Drama

- **Jungle trekking:** In small groups, the children pretend they are enjoying a jungle trekking holiday. Suddenly one member of their party becomes trapped – either in vines and creepers, down a deep pit, or cornered by a ferocious jungle animal – and the rest of the group must try to work out how they are going to free them.

- **Animal charades:** Sit the class in a circle. One at a time, each child mimes or imitates a jungle creature, or performs a charade of a famous jungle character, story or film title. At the end, gather up the sound performers and get them to re-create their animal noises altogether, following your directions to become louder or quieter in a full jungle orchestra!

Extension

- **Jungle tribe:** In larger groups this time, the children prepare, rehearse and perform a scene in which a group of trekkers stumble across a long lost tribe in the middle of a vast jungle. How will they communicate? Will the tribe welcome the visitors or be hostile at first?

Name _____ Date _____

SAVE THE RAINFORESTS!

With a partner, produce a short radio broadcast for a charity, in which you educate listeners about how important the rainforest is and how they can help to preserve it for longer.

You may like to think about:

- why trees are important to the world
- the kinds of animals that live in the rainforest
- the ways in which the rainforest is threatened
- how we can all help (giving money, staying aware of environmental issues).

Write your speech in the space below.

_____

_____

_____

_____

_____

_____

_____

_____

_____

_____

TEACHER'S NOTES

Introduction

- Play the first few seconds of the audio clip and then pause it. Invite the children to suggest what this sound might be.

- Continue to play the whole clip for the class. Discuss the children's first impressions and record any key words and phrases on the board. Establish that this is the sound of military drums and soldiers marching.

Familiarisation

- Replay the sound and then share ideas about what is being spoken in the clip. Can the children identify any orders being given over the top of the drums? What are they?

- Elicit the children's prior knowledge and experience of marching parades like the one in the clip. Where have they seen soldiers on parade? What was it like? Can they describe the experience so that others can see the soldiers in their mind's eye?

Exploration

- Ask the children to imagine they are there, on the scene, as the soldiers go marching past. Brainstorm key descriptive words and phrases to describe the atmosphere of the parade, e.g. *patriotic, exciting, impressive, powerful, proud, uplifting, catchy rhythm, a sense of occasion*, etc.

- Repeat the above exercise, this time viewing the parade through the eyes of a soldier. Words to include could be *tiring, challenging, strict discipline, exhilarating, energetic.*

Audio clip
ROYAL MARINES MARCHING (42 secs)

ACTIVITIES

Speaking

- **Talking partners:** In pairs, the children make a list of the kinds of orders one might expect to hear from a sergeant major (or other caller) on such a parade. They may be able to detect shouts on the clip (see above), or may invent their own appropriate calls. Share ideas at the end and invite the pairs to perform their lists, with the clip playing.

- **Hot seating:** Invite the children to take turns to sit in the 'hot seat' at the front of the classroom. Each volunteer pretends to answer questions in the role of one of the soldiers in the parade, marching or playing a drum. Questions could refer to how long they march for, how often they practise, how difficult it is, how fit one needs to be, etc.

Listening

- **Talk for a minute:** Invite volunteers to stand up and talk for a minute on a given topic related to soldiers. Good topics could include: *boot polish, Great Britain, flags, parades, London, busbies.*

- **'Simon says':** Stand the children in a large circle. Begin by asking them to march on the spot. While they are marching, they must simultaneously follow other instructions that Simon says, including: *put your finger in your ear, hold your nose, close one eye, nod your head, pat your stomach, pat your neighbour's stomach* and so on!

Group Discussion

- **Class discussion:** Why do so many armies give marching displays? What does it say about an army? Does it suggest that they are disciplined, fit, strong, working together or obedient? Share ideas and invite the children to think of other kinds of displays soldiers do/could do to show strength and discipline. You can include acrobatics, formation swimming and sword-dancing.

Drama

- **Group marches:** In groups of five or six, ask the children to prepare, practise and perform a short marching routine. This need not be too sophisticated – just simple marching and turning – but the children must practise it until they are all together, as one. Share and evaluate performances.

Extension

- **Uniforms around the world:** In pairs or small groups, the children research military uniforms around the world. Can they find at least 10 different national forces that have recognisably different uniforms? You may allow the children to use a range of ICT media and library resources. Share and discuss designs at the end.

Name _____ Date _____

RADIO COMMENTARY

Imagine you are a radio reporter at the marching parade that you can hear on the clip. It is a major annual event, involving hundreds of soldiers, all marching in step before the Queen.

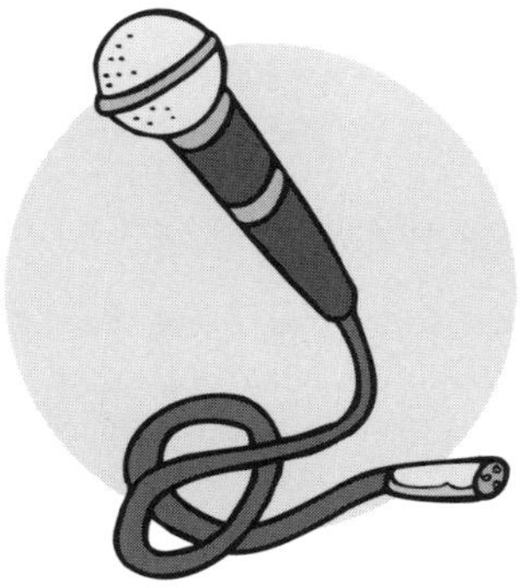

Your task is to describe for the listeners the atmosphere of the big parade. Picture the scene in your mind's eye, then describe the sights and sounds as if you were there.

After writing your report, present your radio broadcast as your teacher plays the sound of the soldiers on parade.

_____

_____

_____

_____

_____

_____

_____

_____

_____

_____

TEACHER'S NOTES

Introduction

- Play the short audio clip and discuss the children's first reactions to the sound. Record any key words and phrases on the board.

- Replay the clip and invite the children to suggest who might be making this sound, and why.

Familiarisation

- Begin a class discussion on the sort of noises we make when we are hurt. List key words on the board that capture these sounds, for example: *ouch, ow, oo!, huh, ooff, aagh!* and so on. You may wish to make it clear that swearing is not acceptable!

- Elicit the children's experiences of suffering minor injuries such as stubbing toes or banging knees. What strategies do we have to cope with these? Is it a quick rub and saying 'never mind'? When accidents happen should we dwell on them, or soldier on?

Exploration

- Replay the clip and invite the children to suggest how old this person might be. How can we tell? Discuss tones and pitches of voice.

- Listen to the sound again and invite the children to suggest what could have happened to the person in the clip.

Audio clip
MALE OW AS IF HIT (01 secs)

ACTIVITIES

 Speaking

- **Talking pairs:** In pairs, the children discuss and make lists of verbs that can be used to describe a minor accident. Good examples are: *stubbing, catching, cutting, knocking, clipping, bashing, bumping.* Share and evaluate work at the end of the activity.

- **Hot seating:** Invite the children to take turns to sit in the 'hot seat' at the front of the classroom. Each person must answer questions from the class in the role of the person in the audio clip, explaining what happened to them and how they felt at the time.

Listening

- **Guess the sound:** In groups, or as a whole class, invite children to take turns to think up a sound of some sort that is an exclamation to show an emotion. The others must guess what they are feeling or what has happened, for example: *sigh* (tired), *laugh* (amused), *shriek* (frightened), *wow!* (amazed).

 Group Discussion

- **Class discussion:** What do we learn from having accidents? Do we always remember not to make the same mistake again? Are we especially careful next time, or do we never learn?

- **Group discussion:** In groups, the children discuss and write down reasons why accidents happen. Some starting points are: *rushing a job, not taking proper precautions, taking one's eye of the job in hand, not looking where we are going* and so on. Share the groups' findings at the end. Try to establish what is the most common cause of an accident.

Drama

- **Group plays:** In small groups, or pairs, invite the children to prepare, rehearse and perform a short sketch which contains the sound in the clip. The play must make sense of the sound, placing it in a context. Share and evaluate performances at the end.

Extension

- **Sound engineers:** In larger groups this time, ask the children to work together to prepare one or more sketches that involve a series of different sounds, provided by two or three members of the group who act as sound engineers 'off stage'. The actors may mime the entire play and the engineers must add the sound effects as the action unfolds. You may wish to prescribe the theme, such as 'haunted house' with sound effects including: *creaking doors, shouts, whispers, shrieks, wind howling*, etc.

Name _____ Date _____

LISTEN UP!

For this activity you will need to watch television!

Watch a clip from a film or cartoon for about 15 minutes. During this time, listen out for sound effects that have been added to the drama. Write them down as you hear them.

You may hear sounds like:

- wind and rain
- footsteps
- machines operating

- moving vehicles
- doors closing
- people talking.

Share your list with the rest of the class. You'll be surprised how many sound effects there are in every film!

Sound number	Description
1	_____
2	_____
3	_____
4	_____
5	_____
6	_____
7	_____
8	_____
9	_____
10	_____

TEACHER'S NOTES

Introduction

• Play the first few seconds of the audio clip and then pause it. Invite the children to suggest what is making this sound.

• Continue to play the whole clip for the class. Establish that this is the sound of water surging in somewhere, perhaps in a cave near the coast.

Familiarisation

• Replay the clip and invite the children to suggest words and phrases (verbs mainly) to describe the sound of the waves, e.g. *surging, pushing, gushing, forcing, lashing*. You may wish to record these on a mind-map on the board.

• Elicit the children's prior knowledge and experience of coastal caves and tides. Share experiences and discuss how dangerous the sea can be if one is caught out by a rising tide.

Exploration

• Play the audio clip once again; explore words and phrases that capture the atmosphere of this clip, as the children see and feel the location in their mind's eye. These could include; *rugged, windswept, hard, natural, unforgiving, unstoppable, wild.*

• Ask the children to explore other possibilities for where and how this sound is being made, for example: wind on Mars, radio interference, a glacier moving, a hurricane, demolition work of some kind. Record these on the board and then discuss what these sounds have in common (e.g. *loud, destructive, battering, fierce, uncontrollable*).

Audio clip
WATER SURGING IN CAVE (2 mins)

ACTIVITIES

Speaking

• **Talking pairs:** In pairs, ask the children to write, rehearse and perform a short narration, poem or commentary that could be recited over the sound clip. For example, it could be the opening narration to a sea story, a poem about waves or a description of a cave.

• **Word tennis:** Invite two volunteers to sit on chairs opposite one another at the front. The first player 'serves' by calling out an adjective that describes the sound (this may be from the opening session above). The second player 'returns' with a different word, and so on until someone falters through hesitation or repetition.

Listening

• **Sound simulation:** In pairs, or small groups, encourage the children to attempt to simulate the audio clip, recreating the sound they hear with nothing but their own voices. Listen to, and evaluate, their attempts. Play the clip once again and assess which group sounds the most similar. They will need to listen carefully to the clip and notice the changes in speed, tone and volume as the waves rise and fall.

Group Discussion

• **Class discussion:** How destructive can the sea be? How powerful is it? Begin a discussion about the strength of the sea and the ferocity with which it can strike. Elicit the children's knowledge of natural disasters linked to tidal movement and clarify any queries which they may have.

Drama

• **Group plays:** In small groups, the children prepare, rehearse and perform a short scene in which they find themselves trapped in a cave, as the tide is coming in. How will they cope? Can they escape, or attract someone's attention back on the beach? Play the audio clip as they act out their scene.

• **Group dance:** Again in small groups, or in pairs, the children prepare, rehearse and perform a short dance sequence in which they try to simulate the movement of the waves, as they lash and swirl and surge. Play the audio clip and watch the group dances. Discuss together how we might capture most effectively the mood and feel of the waves through dance.

Extension

• **Group playscripts:** In small groups, the children collaborate on a group play, written, directed and performed by themselves and set on or near the sea. They may be either pirates smuggling goods, naval heroes in battle or brave explorers. Play the clip again, watch and evaluate the performances.

SHIP'S LOG

Write an excerpt from a ship's log (diary) describing a terrible storm and the day when everyone thought the sea would swallow them up.

Practise reading your diary aloud and then recite it in class. Evaluate each other's work. Who has managed most successfully to capture the atmosphere on board the ship?

_____

_____

_____

_____

_____

_____

_____

_____

_____

_____

_____

_____

OPPORTUNITIES FOR CROSS-CURRICULAR LINKS TO QCA SCHEMES OF WORK (DfES Standards Site) in Mind's Eye Y4

Mind's Eye Y4 Unit IMAGES 1-20	Cross-curricular links (QCA Schemes of work)
AIR RESCUE	**Geography:** Unit 23 Investigating coasts; **Citizenship:** Unit 04 People who help us
BALLOON RACE	**Science:** Unit 5C Gases around us; Unit 6E: Forces in action; **Citizenship:** Unit 01 Taking part; Unit 11 What's the news?
BULL RUN	**Citizenship:** Unit 01 Choices; **ICT:** Unit 1C The information around us; Unit 2C: Finding information.
CARNIVAL	**Art and Design:** Unit 5C Talking textiles; **ICT:** Unit 2C Finding information; **Citizenship:** Unit 05 Living in diverse world; Unit 02 Choices
CHIMPANZEE	**Citizenship:** Unit 01 Taking part; **ICT:** Unit 2C Finding information
EGYPTIAN TOMB	**History:** Unit 10 What can we find out about ancient Egypt from what has survived? **Art and Design:** Unit 2C Can buildings speak?
EVACUEES	**History:** Unit 9 What was it like for children in the second world war? **ICT:** Unit 2C Finding information; **Citizenship:** Unit 11 In the media – what's the news?
ICEBERG	**Geography:** Unit 7 Weather around the world; Unit 24 Passport to the world; **Science:** Unit 4B Habitats; Unit 4C Keeping warm; **Citizenship:** Unit 01 Choices
MINESHAFT	**Science:** Unit 3D Rocks and soils; **History:** Unit 13 How has life in Britain changed since 1948?
MOSQUE	**Art and Design:** Unit 2C Can buildings speak?; **RE:** Unit 6B Worship and community: what is the role of the mosque?; Unit 2D Visiting a place of worship
PALACE	**Art and Design:** Unit 2C Can buildings speak?; **Citizenship:** Unit 01 Taking part
PIANO PLAYING	**Music:** Unit 6 What's the score? – Exploring instruments and symbols
SITTING ALONE	**Citizenship:** Unit 01 Taking part; Unit 02 Choices; **RE:** Unit 6A Worship and community
SKIER	**PE:** Unit 19 Outdoor and adventurous activities; **Geography:** Unit 15 The mountain environment; Unit 19 How and where do we spend out time?; **ICT:** Unit 2C Finding information
SNOWY TRACK	**Geography:** Unit 7 Weather around the world; **Science:** Unit 4B Habitats
SPIRALS AND SHADOWS	**ICT:** Unit 6A Multimedia presentation; **Art and Design:** Unit 3B Investigating pattern
STONE CIRCLE	**History:** Unit 18 What was it like to live here in the past?; **Science:** Unit 3D Rocks and soils; **Art and Design:** Unit 2C Can buildings speak?
SUBMARINE	**Geography:** Unit 23 Investigating coasts; **ICT:** Unit 4D Collecting and presenting information
SWIMMERS	**Science:** Unit 4B Habitats; **Geography:** Unit 4 Going to the seaside; Unit 19 How and where do we spend our time?; Unit 23 Investigating coasts
X-RAY VISION	**Citizenship:** Unit 08 How do rules and laws affect me?; Unit 09 Respect for property

Mind's Eye Y4 Unit SOUNDS 1-10	Cross-curricular links (QCA Schemes of work)
AFRICAN DRUMS	**Music:** Unit 4 Exploring pulse and rhythm; Unit 6 What's the score? – Exploring instruments and symbols; **PE:** Unit 9 Dance activities (4); **Design and Technology:** Unit 5A Musical instruments
DOLPHIN CALLS	**Citizenship:** Unit 03 Animals and us; **Geography:** Unit 8 Improving the environment; **Science:** Unit 4B Habitats
ELEPHANT	**Citizenship:** Unit 03 Animals and us; **Geography:** Unit 8 Improving the environment
EMERGENCY	**Citizenship:** Unit 04 People who help us – the local police; Unit 11 In the media – what's the news? **Geography:** Unit 12 Should the high street be closed to traffic?
FLYING SAUCER	**Science:** Unit 1F Sound and hearing; Unit 5F Changing sounds
HOWLING WIND	**Geography:** Unit 7 Weather around the world; Unit 18 Connecting ourselves to the world
JUNGLE	**Geography:** Unit 8 Improving the environment; **Citizenship:** Unit 03 Animals and us; **Science:** Unit 4B Habitats
MARCHING	**ICT:** Unit 2C Finding information; Unit 6A Multimedia presentation; **History:** Unit 17 What are we remembering on Remembrance Day?
OUCH!	**Science:** Unit 5F Changing sounds; **Citizenship:** Unit 02 Choices; Unit 09 Respect for property; **Music:** Unit 2 Sounds interesting
WATER SURGING	**Geography:** Unit 1 Water; Unit 23 Investigating coasts; **PE:** Unit 9 Dance activities (4)